CHAPTER 1
Why You Need This Book!

You might have seen different books out there about sous vide cooking, yet this is the main book that is composed explicitly to make you a sous vide master utilizing your Anova Immersion circulator. As you may definitely know, the Anova is the ideal device for at home sous vide greatness and this book will offer master tips and plans to capitalize on your Anova. But that's not all. We're likewise going to talk about the science behind why the Anova is the absolute most ideal choice for at home sous vide cooking. You will figure out how to give your Anova something to do to make everything from breakfast to dessert utilizing the safest

and most dependable cooking strategy ever invented.

Get More Out of Your Anova Immersion Circulator

If you've effectively bought the Anova Immersion Circulator you are likely keen on the study of sous vide. Quite a while back, proficient gourmet specialists running high volume kitchens ran into an issue: How to rapidly serve food to a café loaded with clients rapidly and cooked appropriately. They coincidentally found an astonishing thought: Cook food to the ideal temperature and afterward finish on the barbecue or under a grill depending on the situation. Unexpectedly high volume kitchens could at long last stay aware of the bustling speed of an enormous café. But they discovered that they could also cook nearly anything using this method. It required a significant stretch of time to get on, however home cooks are presently understanding that this technique that has since a long time ago kept occupied cafés moving along as planned can be utilized at home to make suppers effectively and cooked flawlessly. In this book we're demonstrating that sous vide isn't only for the geniuses and it isn't only for making the ideal steak. We will open the genuine force of your Anova Immersion Circulator.

"Street-Wise" Pro Tips for Amazing Sous Vide Meals

Finally, the insider facts of ace gourmet specialists are accessible to home culinary experts and we will clarify every one of the intricate details of how to make the most astonishing dinners utilizing your Anova to cook sous vide. Our industry-tried tips will transform you into a specialist in a matter of moments. We'll cover everything from how to get the best seal, to how you can utilize exact time and temperature utilizing your Anova to make dishes you might have just envisioned about. Need tumble off-the-bone grill ribs yet you don't have a space for a smoker? Not an issue assuming you follow our restrictive tips to benefit from your sous vide experience.

Over 100 Delicious Sous Vide Recipes!

Not just will this book train you the procedures behind utilizing the Anova to get the best sous vide results, it will likewise give more than 100 plans that will encourage you how to make astonishing vegetable, chicken, fish, pork, hamburger, sheep, and pastries, all utilizing the sous vide strategy. Notwithstanding the plans, you will likewise get familiar with the mysteries behind a few incredible rubs and flavors that will make your dishes truly come alive.

How to Use Your Anova Immersion Circulator

One of the fundamental benefits of sous vide cooking is that you can begin cooking and not need to continue to beware of your food the entire time. Not at all like business sous vide units, the Anova is intended for simple home use. Truth be told, all you really want other than the Anova is a holder to hold sufficient water to lower your food, and a gadget to vacuum seal the nourishment for cooking. For fixing we suggest the Foodsaver. To work your Anova, just utilize the cinch screw to connect the unit to the side of a holder and empty sufficient water into the compartment to enough cover the food. The Anova has a most extreme fill line to tell you where to quit filling. Plug in the Anova, and utilizing the temperature wheel on the presentation screen, set the temperature you need. Press the set button and the Anova will start circling and warming the water. To change to an alternate temperature, just utilize the wheel to change temperatures and press set once more. It truly is that easy.

It's The ONLY Sous Vide Cookbook You Will Ever Need

Not just does this book offer astonishing plans and the science behind sous vide cooking, it will give you all that you want, from the planning to the real cooking, to make astounding sous vide dishes that will save time and energy. Best of all, your dishes will come out perfectly every time. Therefore top culinary experts all around the world have been utilizing sous vide cooking for a really long time. The Anova is the business driving drenching circulator justifiably. It is economical, simple to utilize, and 100 percent precise. Taking into account how simple the Anova is to utilize, it's no big surprise that sous vide cooking is just turning out to be more famous with home cooks. Never again stress over finished or half-cooking your food. The Anova guarantees that regardless you are cooking, it will be amazing each time.

CHAPTER 2
Why Use The Anova for Sous Vide

It's All About Even Temperature

No matter the thing you're cooking, whether it's fish, a perfectly marbled steak, or fragile pastries, getting incredible outcomes is tied in with controlling the temperature, and several degrees totally will have a significant effect. The Anova capacities by flowing the cooking water and warming it to an exceptionally exact temperature. Along these lines, all that you cook will be raised to this precise temperature and not a degree pretty much. There is, in a real sense, no

cooking strategy on Earth that offers this degree of accuracy, which is the reason proficient gourmet experts the world over depend on sous vide cooking to keep up with the best expectations of cuisine.

Plan Meals Ahead of Time and Freeze Them

With the bustling speed of life nowadays, planning heavenly home prepared suppers consistently can be a test. But with a vacuum sealer, you can prepare complete meals that can be frozen for months. Essentially add each of your fixings to the sack, seal it, pop it in the cooler, and afterward cook it the sous vide way utilizing the Anova at whatever point you're prepared. As a result of the even hotness that Anova offers, it prepares food substantially more equally than a microwave. Furthermore on the grounds that it utilizes a lot of lower temperatures than a traditional broiler, you can cook securely without oversight. At the point when you pair your Anova drenching circulator with a vacuum-sealer, you can cook nearly anything effectively and rapidly, with scrumptious outcomes each time.

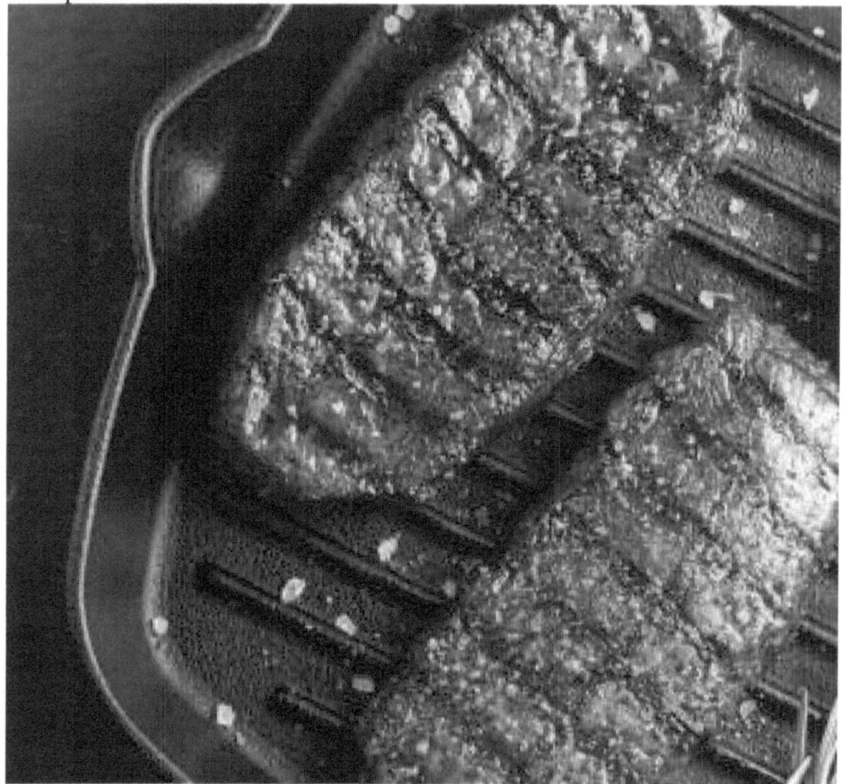

Sous Vide Locks In the Flavor.

Sous vide is French for "under vacuum" and it is this vacuum seal that makes two major benefits: First, it implies that your food gets prepared equally with no air inside the sack to make temperature issues. It likewise implies that flavors or marinades have consistent contact with whatever you are cooking. This truly presses the flavors straightforwardly into the nourishment for extra delectable dishes.

The Anova Provides the Most Reliable Method for Perfectly Cooked Meals

Let's face it, the majority of us aren't proficient gourmet specialists. But that doesn't mean we don't want to make a wide variety of excellent food. Cooking can be a test, and perhaps the most troublesome viewpoint is realizing the way in which hot you really want to cook, and for how long. Fortunately, the Anova Immersion Circulator is intended to take all of the mystery out of setting up your beloved dinners. By rigorously controlling the temperature, you can ensure ideal outcomes without long stretches of training. What's more with a great vacuum sealer available, you realize that your suppers are preparing evenly.

It's Perfect for Those with Busy Schedules

Most of us can't bear to spend our entire day remaining at the oven. Furthermore in the wake of a difficult day, nobody anticipates spending the remainder of the evening in the kitchen making supper. All things considered, on account of the Anova, you don't need to. Numerous things like steaks and fish can be cook Thusus vide in under 60 minutes. So, you should simply seal your food in a pack, set the Anova to the legitimate temperature, drop it in the water shower, and unwind. There's no compelling reason to determine the status of your food. The Anova will accomplish basically everything for you. But let's say you feel like some barbecue pulled pork for dinner. All things considered, just set your Anova and pop it in the water shower toward the beginning of the day and let it cook day in and day out. The Anova is entirely protected to use without oversight so you can make those scrumptious tedious suppers while you continue ahead with the remainder of your day.

It's The Healthiest and Safest Cooking Method

Since there is no immediate contact with a hotness source, you can keep away from a great deal of the overabundance fat and oil that is utilized in regular cooking. This implies that you can make better dinners all the more regularly. But that's not the only health benefit of sous vide cooking. Since you're not utilizing high hotness, there isn't the danger of losing supplements that are annihilated at higher temperatures. Sous vide is additionally the most secure cooking technique since there are no high hotness sources. The Anova is intended to run for amazingly extensive stretches of time with no oversight required, so you can have a good sense of reassurance cooking while you're not home, or overnight.

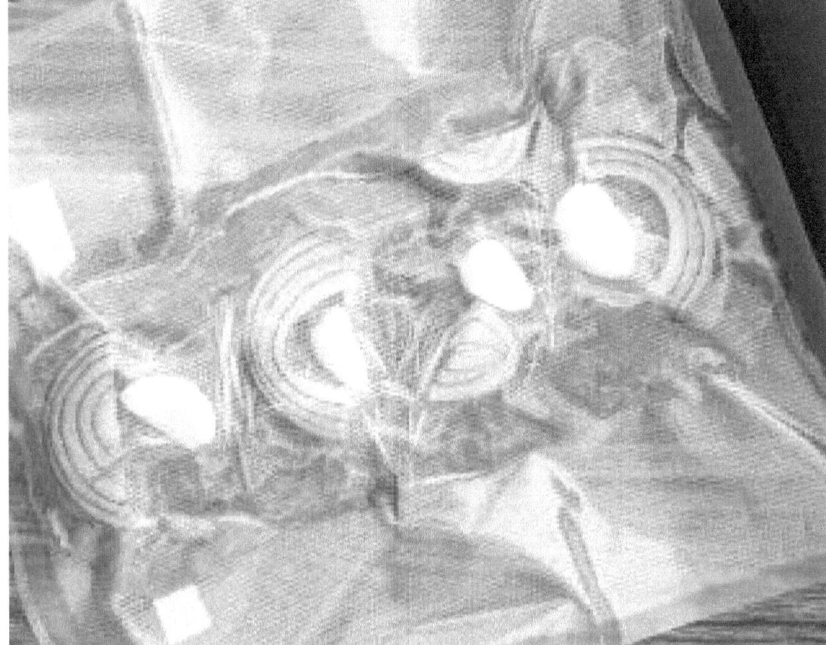

CHAPTER 3
The Surprising Health Benefits of Sous Vide Cooking

Preserve Those Nutrients!

Everyone is worried about getting appropriate sustenance, yet what you cannot deny is that sure cooking strategies can really obliterate a portion of the indispensable supplements that we really want. Many sorts of food, including meats and vegetables can lose a lot of their supplements while being cooked over high hotness. A few fat based supplements can essentially separate and become less valuable, while others are lost as the juices cook out of the food. With sous vide cooking, in any case, you don't need to stress over losing those valuable supplements. Since sous vide utilizes a lot of lower temperatures, the supplements stay unblemished. What's more since the juices are completely held inside the vacuum fixed pack, they don't have anyplace to go.

No Additional Oil Needed

Using conventional cooking strategies, it's almost difficult to cook without the utilization of fat. And keeping in mind that specific oils, like olive oil, do have medical advantages, others, similar to spread, are simply adding pointless fat to your eating regimen. Since food prepared with the sous vide strategy doesn't contact a hot surface, no oil is needed in the cooking system. What's more since studies have shown that oils warmed to high temperature can cause an assortment of medical problems, sous vide cooking totally kills this concern.

Plan Healthy Meals in Advance

Eating healthy every day can be a challenge mainly because of the time involved to prepare food. Sometimes it just feels easier to order a pizza or stop by the fast food place on the way home. But what if you could stock your freezer with healthy meals that you could prepare at a moment's notice? By spending some time to prepare healthy meals in advance and then vacuum sealing the raw ingredients, you can have months' worth of healthy options ready to go. Considering how easy sous vide cooking is using the Anova, you really don't have any excuse not to eat healthy.

Using The Anova to Sous Vide Ensures Food Safety

It may appear to be odd to prepare food at such a low temperature, yet the idea

behind sous vide cooking is to bring the food just to the specific wanted temperature to forestall over or half-cooking. To This end sous-vide has gotten on so well with both expert gourmet specialists just as home cooks. With no mystery, and no compelling reason to counsel a thermometer, you can be guaranteed that your food will come out cooked flawlessly, yet you can likewise have confidence that it is cooked to a protected temperature. This, joined with the way that the food is vacuum fixed and not at risk for being sullied by normal kitchen microbes, protects a protected and dependable cooking experience.

Only Use Plastic that is Safe to Cook With

You've presumably caught wind of the risks of food coming into contact with specific plastics, and the synthetics that can advance into your food. Indeed, fortunately Foodsaver's vacuum seal packs are planned explicitly to be presented to both hotness and cold with no wellbeing hazards regularly connected with plastic. Foodsaver sacks are BPA free and microwave safe so you can experience absolute harmony of psyche when utilizing them to freeze, sous vide, or simply warm in the microwave.

CHAPTER 4
How to Cook Anything Sous Vide

The Science of Sous Vide

Sous vide is French for "under vacuum" and has become progressively well known for two reasons: It is amazingly dependable, and it produces delicate, impeccably prepared food without the problem of customary cooking strategies. With sous vide there is no mystery regarding whether your food is being cooked to the appropriate temperature, and no concerns that it very well may be finished or underdone. Food is fixed in a vacuum tight sack and lowered in a shower of water that is circled and kept at the legitimate cooking temperature utilizing a sous vide inundation circulator.

Sous Vide Equipment

It's actual that sous vide cooking requires some extra hardware, however the incredible thing about sous vide is that you can utilize precisely the same gear to cook everything. As the term sous vide proposes, the main piece of the cycle is a decent vacuum seal. Other than this, you will require the Anova inundation circulator to warm your water shower, and a compartment adequately enormous to lower anything you desire to cook.

What is a Sous Vide Immersion Circulator?

Excellent inquiry! There are many sous-vide units accessible nowadays and a large number of them are extraordinary for home use. Contingent upon how much food you're intending to cook, you can settle on how strong a sous vide unit you will require. The Anova Immersion Circulator is cheap and works really hard concocting for to eight individuals all at once. Essentially connect the sous vide unit to the side of a compartment that can hold sufficient water to appropriately lower your food (around 12 quarts) and set it to the ideal temperature. The sous vide unit will tell you when it has arrived at that temperature, and afterward it's simply a question of putting your vacuum fixed food in the water and waiting.

CHAPTER 5
How the Anova Immersion Circulator Works

- Your Anova Immersion Circulator really couldn't be easier to use.
- You will notice that there is a clamp on the unit that can be fit to many types of containers. Simply mount the Anova on the side of the container and turn the clamp screw until it is tight.
- Fill the container to the fill line on the metal part of the Anova and press the power button. The display should light up with the temperature in either Celsius or Fahrenheit and this can be changed by pressing the "select" button.
- For your convenience, this book lists all temperatures in both Celsius and Fahrenheit.
- Simply roll the dial on the display to the desired temperature and press the "set" button. The circulator will activate, and the water will begin to heat.
- Once it has reached the proper temperature, the Anova will beep to let you know that it's time to cook.

Sous Vide Isn't Just for Meat

As we'll examine later in the plans, sous vide cooking is a phenomenal approach to guaranteeing that your meat doles come out flawlessly without stressing over how hot or how long to cook, yet what you cannot deny is that the sous vide strategy can cook pretty much anything flawlessly. Any vegetables that you would have either simmered or steamed can be fixed into a vacuum-fixed sack for a fast and simple sous vide that secures every one of the significant supplements. Also thusly, your veggies are holding on and prepared to eat at whatever point you are.

Sous Vide for Breakfast

Who isn't a fan of a perfectly cooked Eggs Benedict? But poached eggs can take a lot of practice to get just right. Since your sous vide keeps a consistent temperature consistently, making the ideal poached egg is pretty much as simple as breaking an egg. A similar technique can be utilized to make delicate bubbled and hard bubbled eggs also. Simply drop the egg into the water shower and set a kitchen clock. Your eggs will be the specific consistency you need each time.

Make Your Favorite Slow-Cooked Barbecue With Your Anova

If you're a fan of good old fashioned barbecue, you know that it's not easy. You'll need a smoker, a lot of time, and you need to check it constantly to make sure it's hot enough, or not too hot. It's pretty much a full time job. I know it sounds crazy, but what if you could make all of your favorite slow-cooked barbecue foods sous vide with hardly any work? As we'll discuss

later in the book, a portion of these plans require a long cooking time, however with a sous vide you will not need to continue to beware of your food. You can securely begin cooking in the first part of the day, go to work, and eat sitting tight for you when you return home. And best of all, your food will be succulent and tender every single time.

CHAPTER 6
Pro Tips to Make Perfect Sous Vide Creations

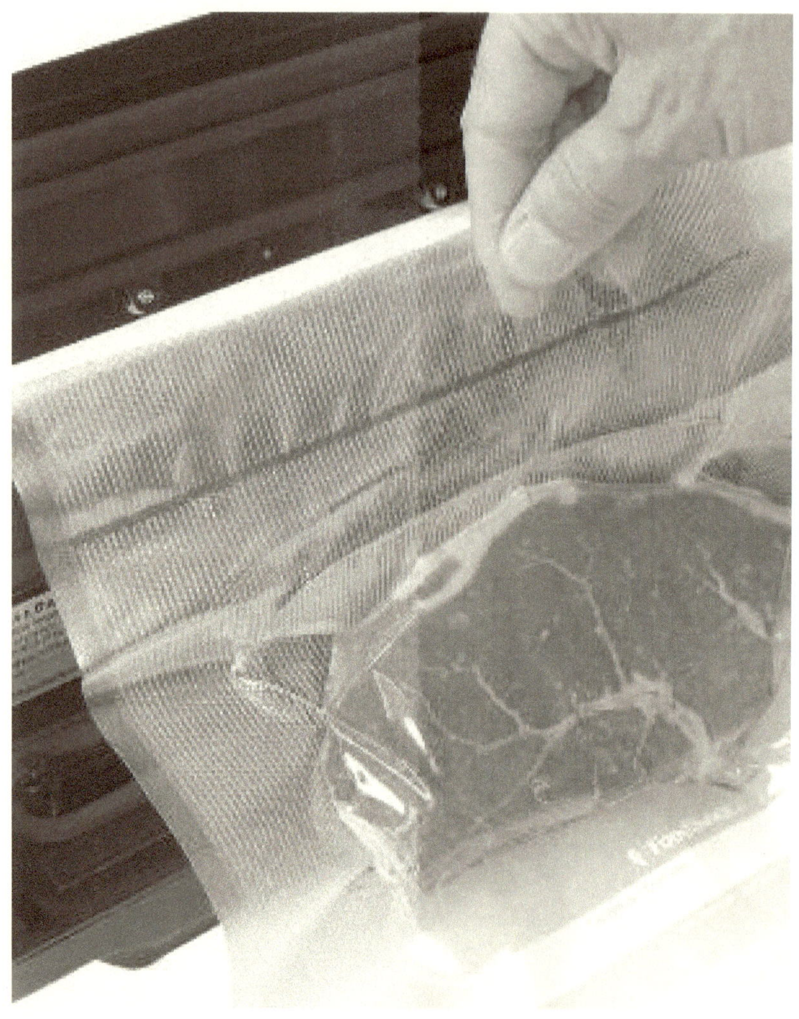

A Great Sear is a Way to Add Flavor

You've gotten your food to the ideal temperature, yet what's straightaway? Indeed, certain food varieties like vegetables and fish are frequently prepared to eat right out of the sack. But things like beef or chicken can benefit from one more step. In the event that you're

making a decent New York Strip steak, your sous vide has cooked within to whatever temperature you like, yet a large portion of us like a pleasant dull burn on a steak. When you're content with the inward temperature, get a dish (ideally a cast iron skillet) hot with the eventual result of smoking with a tablespoon of vegetable oil. Drop your steak in the prospect several minutes on each side to accomplish a pleasant dim burn. To improve the singe further, take a stab at placing a tablespoon of margarine in the container while burning for a significantly more obscure, crisper outside. The high hotness will singe the outside pleasantly, however within will remain delicious and rare.

With The Anova There's No Need to Rest Meat

Generally, when cooking things like hamburger, you should rest it in the wake of cooking. Contingent upon how huge a piece of meat you have, this time could

range somewhere in the range of ten minutes for a normal steak, to about an hour for a rib broil. The explanation meat needs to rest is to give the cooler inside temperature of the meat time to try and out with the more smoking outer temperature of the outer layer of the meat. Permitting the meat to rest guarantees that the juices inside the meat will be completely retained and not lost when the meat is cut. At the point when meat is cooked sous vide, this contrast between the inside and outside temperatures doesn't exist, and that implies meat cooked sous vide can be served right out of the sack. Or then again right out of the container assuming you're burning it.

Cook Low and Slow for Fall-Off-The-Bone Meats

We've effectively talked about the way that cooking sous vide is an incredible way to

make your beloved grill dishes in your kitchen without the problem of utilizing a smoker, yet how does this truly work? Meats like pork shoulder and brisket are heavenly, yet to get that tumble off the bone surface they must be cooked for quite a while. This implies that you either need to smoke them at low temperatures or keep them in the broiler day in and day out. This can be interesting assuming that you have a bustling timetable. But with sous vide cooking you can safely cook food all day without supervision. To make amazing pork ribs at home, season the outside of the meat with your cherished rub (we'll speak more with regards to rubs later), seal it with your vacuum sealer, and change your Anova Immersion Circulator to 165 degrees. Then submerge the ribs in the water and cook for twelve hours.

Never Cook Too Low for Too Long

Sous vide cooking is one of the simplest and most secure ways of cooking nearly anything, however assuming food is prepared at too low a temperature for a really long time, you risk food borne disease. Food sources like fish are best at around 120-125 degrees, however they just need around a thirty minutes in the sous vide to cook appropriately. After over three hours at such a low temperature, microscopic organisms can start to duplicate and turn into a wellbeing hazard. A decent guideline is: Foods that are best at a low temp like fish should just cook for a brief time frame (under three hours), and food sources that need a long cook time should be cooked at high temperatures (165 degrees and up). In the event that you adhere to these fundamental rules you shouldn't at any point need to stress over your food being 100 percent protected to eat.

Equipment Recommendations

We suggest the Anova Precision Cooker since it is reasonable and minimal enough to store without any problem. It has sufficient ability to warm and course an enormous volume of water, however it isn't quite so cumbersome as models ordinarily utilized in eateries. We likewise suggest a vacuum sealer-Foodsaver. It is the most awesome item for fixing your food, yet with so many models accessible, it tends to be hard to tell which one is appropriate for you. For home use, we suggest the Foodsaver V2244 which should offer the adaptability to seal everything except is as yet reasonable and won't occupy an excessive amount of space in your kitchen.

CHAPTER 7
How to Store Your Leftover Sous Vide Items

General Storage

The most ideal way to store your food is to utilize the Foodsaver (or other brand of vacuum sealer). Since you as of now utilize one for your sous vide, why not use it for capacity too?

The extraordinary thing about the Foodsaver is that it very well may be utilized to seal everything from meats and veggies to dry products. With solid without bpa packs, you can seal anything and experience the harmony of psyche that it will be secure for extremely significant stretch of time. The top notch heat seal is the way to newness since it doesn't corrupt after some time. With the Foodsaver, whenever it's fixed, it stays sealed.

The Foodsaver Makes Storage a Breeze

We've effectively examined the upsides of cooking utilizing the Foodsaver to vacuum seal food, however it is, point of fact, the absolute most ideal way to store extras either in the cooler or cooler. Just follow similar strides with extra food, and store in the cooler for a really long time. Foodsaver packs are likewise simple to compose on, so there's no mystery with regards to how long something has been in the cooler. Also on the grounds that your food has as of now been cooked to the ideal temperature, it is totally protected to reseal prepared nourishment for freezing.

Use the Foodsaver to Turn Tonight's Leftovers into Next Week's Dinner

Since the Foodsaver alongside the sous vide technique makes cooking so natural, why not make additional nourishment for those occasions when you simply don't have the opportunity to cook yet at the same time need a heavenly home prepared supper. Assuming you prepare and sous vide more that you're wanting to eat, simply reseal the extras with your Foodsaver in a similar sack you used to cook, and pop it in the cooler. At the point when you're prepared to utilize those extras, either defrost in the refrigerator or just set the frozen pack back in your sous-vide at 165 degrees for about 60 minutes. You presently have one more impeccably prepared feast with no work.

Store Your Sous Vide Items Together or Separately

Most individuals will more often than not store their extras in independent compartments. Meat in one,

pureed potatoes in another. With the Foodsaver you can seal your extras independently or make total suppers that are prepared to warm up at whatever point. It resembles a definitive TV supper that you made yourself.

CHAPTER 8
APPETIZERS

Sous Vide Duck Leg Confit

SERVINGS: 2 | PREP TIME: 20 MINUTES | COOK TIME: 10-12 HOURS

Duck confit ordinarily requires something like an entire day to get ready yet utilizing your Anova you can make a delectable duck confit with scarcely any work at all.

INGREDIENTS:

1 tablespoon dried
thyme 3 straight leaves
1 cup salt
2 duck legs,
frenched 6
tablespoons duck fat
Salt and newly ground pepper, to
taste 3 tablespoons duck fat

INSTRUCTIONS:

1. Crush the dried thyme and narrows leaves in the salt until they are equitably blended. Generously cover the duck legs with the salt blend and spot in the cooler somewhere around 12, and up to 36 hours.
2. Remove the duck legs from the fridge and flush off the salt with cold water.
3. Set your Anova unit to 167F/75C.
4. Place the duck legs in a vacuum-fixed pack with 4 tablespoons of the duck fat and seal.
5. Once the water shower has arrived at the right temperature, place the fixed sack in the water.
6. Cook the duck legs for 10 to 12 hours.
7. Remove the sack from the water and eliminate the duck legs from the bag.
8. When you are prepared to serve, heat a skillet with 2 tablespoons of duck fat and burn until the skin is crispy.
9. Just prior to serving, in a hot dish, warm the excess 2 tablespoons duck fat. Add the duck legs and burn until the skin is crisp.
10. This cycle can likewise be utilized to cook duck bosoms. Simply change the temperature of the water shower to 135F/57C and cook for 45 minutes.

Nutritional Info: Calories: 665, Sodium: 82mg, Dietary Fiber: 1.3g, Total Fat: 62g; Total Carbs: 3.1g, Protein: 22g.

Soft Sous Vide Goose Egg

SERVINGS: 2 | PREP TIME: 30 MINUTES | COOK TIME: 2-1/2 HOURS

This debauched treat is a brilliant beginning to any dinner, and the rich polenta can likewise be utilized in numerous different plans with astonishing results.

INGREDIENTS

For the Polenta:

1 cup coarse ground polenta 6 tablespoons spread, partitioned 4 cups entire milk
1 cup parmesan, grated

Sea salt and newly ground dark pepper to taste

For the Pancetta and Eggs:
4 goose eggs that are comparative in size (the size of the eggs will influence their cooking time)
8 cuts of pancetta, ideally very thin
4 small bunches of your beloved greens, threw with some extra-virgin olive oil A couple of portions of ocean salt
Freshly ground parmesan

INSTRUCTIONS

For the Polenta:
1. First, top off your water shower and set your Anova unit to 190F/87C.
2. While the water is heating up, place the polenta, margarine, and milk into a vacuum-fixed sack. Your vacuum sealer should eliminate all of the air from around the food.
3. Submerge the pack and cook for 2 to 2-1/2 hours. While the polenta cooks, grind 8 ounces of Parmesan cheese.
4. Remove the sack from the water broiler and pour quickly over the Parmesan cheddar in an enormous bowl. Throw the fixings and season with salt and pepper.

For the Pancetta and Eggs:
1. Using a similar water shower, change your Anova unit to 167F/75C. It'll take a short time for the water to cook down so you can likewise add a digit of cold water to the shower to accelerate the interaction. You can keep the polenta warm in the water shower while you cook the pancetta and eggs. The normal goose egg should cook for 5 minutes.
2. Gently spot to eggs in the water shower. There is no compelling reason to seal them.
3. While the eggs cook, heat up a cast-iron or treated steel skillet over medium hotness and cook the pancetta until brilliant brown, around 5 to 7 minutes.
4. When sautéed, place pancetta on a plate and cover with a paper towel. Utilizing a couple of utensils, pull the eggs from the water shower, and wash under cool water. Since your eggs are exceptionally delicate, be cautious when breaking them.
5. Spoon polenta onto a plate and spot the egg in the polenta. Top with the firm polenta and present with greens and a liberal tidying of ground Parmesan cheese.

Sous Vide Salmon Gravlax

SERVINGS: 8 | PREP TIME: 30 MINUTES | COOK TIME: 1 HOUR

Gravlax by and large requires quite a while to accomplish delicious relieved salmon, yet you can accelerate the interaction with phenomenal outcomes utilizing your Anova.

INGREDIENTS:

4 tablespoons salt
4 tablespoons sugar
1 teaspoon powdered smoke*
(discretionary) 8 salmon portions

INSTRUCTIONS:

1. Set your Anova unit to 104F/40C.
2. Mix together the salt and sugar, and totally cover the salmon in the dry fix combination. Let sit for 30 minutes, then, at that point, rinse.
3. Put the salmon segments into vacuum-fixed sacks (you can seal them independently or next to each other, however don't stack them).
4. Submerge the packs in the water stove to cook for 45 minutes to 1 hour.
5. Remove the packs from the water shower and chill in an ice water shower for 15 to 20 minutes.
6. Serve as a canapé or with toasted bagels, cream cheddar, onions and tricks for a conventional Scandinavian breakfast.

Sous Vide Herb Butter Shrimp

SERVINGS: 3 | PREP TIME: 10 MINUTES | COOK TIME: 20 MINUTES

Everyone loves shrimp yet cooking them appropriately can be a test. It appears as though they're either finished or half-cooked. Fortunately, cooking shrimp sous vide takes all of the mystery out of impeccably cooked shrimp.

INGREDIENTS:

12 medium stripped
shrimps 1/4 dissolved
butter
1 finely minced
shallot 2 teaspoons
new thyme
1/2 teaspoon ground lemon zest
1 tablespoon lemon juice, for serving

INSTRUCTIONS:

1. Fill your water shower and set your Anova to 125F/51.6C.
2. While the water is coming up to the appropriate temperature, place every one of the fixings in a vacuum-fixed bag.
3. Place the pack in the water shower and cook for 20 minutes. Try not to cook the shrimp longer than 30 minutes for the surface will become mushy.
4. Remove the pack from the water and serve. The shrimp make an incredible starter all alone, or you can throw them with your cherished pasta. They can likewise be chilled and utilized in a salad.

Nutritional Info: Calories: 37, Sodium: 64mg, Dietary Fiber: 0.9g, Total Fat: 1.5g, Total Carbs: 0.9g, Protein: 5.3g.

Sous Vide Prosciutto Wrapped Rabbit

SERVINGS: 4 | PREP TIME: 20 MINUTES | COOK TIME: 5 HOURS

This dish might seem muddled however utilizing your Anova will make arrangement and cooking simpler than you can envision. Intrigue your visitors with something genuinely special and extraordinary.

INGREDIENTS:

1 pound hare rear leg meat, boned, diced
enormous 1/4 pound bacon, diced
1/4 pound pork butt, diced
1/2 teaspoon every coriander, clove, fennel, and juniper berry, finely ground

1/4 cup brandy
1 teaspoon new marjoram, finely hacked
1 teaspoon new thyme, finely slashed 1/2
cup weighty cream
12 slender cuts
prosciutto 4 hare loins
1 tablespoon olive oil
6 to 8 ounces maitake or chanterelle
mushrooms 1 bundle kale, finely chopped
Salt and pepper to taste
4 ounces demi-glace for the sauce

INSTRUCTIONS:

1. Fill your water shower and set Anova unit to 164F/73.5C.
2. In a food processor, grind the bacon, pork butt, bunny rear leg meat and spices. Then, at that point, add the cream, flavors and liquor to the food processor and puree until you have the surface of a mousse.
3. Chill the mousse for 30 minutes so it becomes firm.
4. Place the prosciutto cuts onto of a sheet of cling wrap roughly 12 inches long, so the prosciutto covers and gives a 6-inch wide sheet to work with.
5. Spread the mousse over the sheet of prosciutto making a 1/3-inch thick layer.
6. Place the hare flank in the focal point of the mousse and season softly with salt.
7. Roll the prosciutto around the midsection, so the midsection is presently not noticeable. Eliminate the saran wrap as you go with the goal that the roll stays stable. Then, using a new piece of plastic wrap the roll the whole thing, creating a cylinder. Ensure it is firmly wrapped.
8. Cut a vacuum-seal pack a couple inches longer than the chamber and vacuum seal with your Foodsaver or any vacuum sealer that you have in your kitchen.
9. Place your fixed sack in the water shower and cook for 4 hours. Make an ice shower, and when the sack has gotten done with cooking eliminate from boiling water shower and spot in the ice water to hold it back from cooking any further.
10. While the pack is cooling in the ice shower, heat a skillet on the oven to high hotness. Open up the chamber and spot in the hot skillet, burning on all sides. While you are doing this, heat your broiler to 350

degrees. When the chamber is carmelized place in a simmering
container and spot in the broiler for 6 minutes.

11. While the chamber cooks, heat a skillet over medium high hotness
    with olive oil and sauté the mushrooms and kale until delicate, and
    warm the demi-glace. Season to taste with salt and pepper.
12. Remove chamber from the stove and let rest for ten minutes
    prior to cutting. Present with the mushrooms and kale.

Nutritional Info: Calories: 616, Sodium: 1,368mg, Dietary Fiber: 1.2g, Total
Fat: 35g, Total Carbs: 6.6g, Protein: 63g.

Sous Vide Spinach Artichoke Dip

SERVINGS: 10 | PREP TIME: 15 MINUTES | COOK TIME: 1 HOUR

This simple to make starter is magnificent for engaging or as a bite. It is
best matched with a new French roll and a glass of dry white wine.

INGREDIENTS:

2 cups ground parmesan cheese
10 ounces frozen, hacked spinach
(defrosted) 14 ounces artichoke hearts,
chopped
2/3 cups harsh
cream 1 cup
cream cheddar 1/3
cup mayonnaise
2 teaspoons minced garlic
1 loaf cut into adjusts
Olive oil for brushing

INSTRUCTIONS:

1. Fill your water shower and set your Anova unit to 165F/73.8C.
2. In a medium bowl, join the parmesan cheddar, spinach, and
   artichoke hearts.
3. In another bowl, combine as one the acrid cream, cream
   cheddar, mayonnaise, and garlic.
4. Combine all fixings in a vacuum-fixed pack. When the water shower
   has arrived at the legitimate temperature, place the sack in the water
   shower and cook something like 60 minutes, and up to six hours.

5. When the plunge is practically gotten done, heat your stove to 400 degrees and cut the roll into half-inch-thick rounds.
6. Place the rounds on a baking sheet and brush daintily with olive oil. Place adjusts in the stove for around 15 minutes until daintily browned.
7. Remove the plunge from the water shower and present with toasted baguette.

Nutritional Info: Calories: 260, Sodium: 337mg, Dietary Fiber: 2.9g, Total Fat: 21g, Total Carbs: 10.6g, Protein: 10g.

Tender Sous Vide Buffalo Wings

SERVINGS: 10 | PREP TIME: 15 MINUTES | COOK TIME: 1 HOUR 10 MINUTES

Buffalo wings are generally seared, however for a better wing with tumble off the bone meat and a firm skin, your Anova will give you precisely the flavor you're searching for without profound frying.

INGREDIENTS:

12 chicken wings
1/2 cup universally handy flour
1/4 teaspoon cayenne
pepper 1 scramble garlic
powder
1/4 teaspoon salt
1/4 cup softened
margarine 1/4 cup hot
pepper sauce
1-3/4 tablespoons vegetable oil

INSTRUCTIONS:

1. Fill your water shower and set your Anova unit to 170F/76.6C.
2. In a medium bowl, combine as one the flour, cayenne pepper, garlic powder, and salt.
3. Place the dry blend in a vacuum-fixed pack. Shake the blend and afterward add the chicken wings. Shake again to cover the wings and afterward add the vegetable oil. Seal the sack utilizing your vacuum sealer.

4. Once the water shower has reached to address temperature, place the pack in the water and cook somewhere around 1 hour and up to 4 hours.
5. In another bowl join the softened spread and hot sauce.
6. When you are nearly wrapped up cooking the wings in the water shower heat your broiler to 450 degrees.
7. Remove wings from the water shower and plunge wings in the margarine hot sauce blend so they are covered. Place the wings on a baking sheet and cook in the broiler until the outside of the wings are crispy.
8. Serve with blue cheddar dressing and cut veggies.

Nutritional Info: Calories: 303, Sodium: 225mg, Dietary Fiber: 0g, Total Fat: 18g, Total Carbs: 6g, Protein: 25.8g.

Spicy Ginger Pork Lettuce Wraps

SERVINGS: 12 | PREP TIME: 1 HOUR | COOK TIME: 1-4 HOURS

Lettuce wraps are a light sound other option, and this Asian motivated pork filling packs a lot of flavor without the extra calories.

INGREDIENTS:

3/4 pounds ground pork
1 red ringer pepper, finely
diced 1 garlic clove, minced
1 tablespoon minced stripped
ginger 1 tablespoon Thai sweet
stew sauce 1 tablespoon Asian
fish sauce
1 teaspoon Asian sesame oil
1 tablespoon in addition to 1 teaspoon grapeseed oil
1 (8-ounce) can entire water chestnuts, depleted and
diced 2 scallions, meagerly sliced
2 tablespoons clam sauce
2 tablespoons hacked cilantro
24 enormous lettuce leaves

INSTRUCTIONS:

1. In a medium bowl, consolidate the ground pork with the chime pepper, garlic, ginger, stew sauce, fish sauce, sesame oil, and 1

tablespoon of the grapeseed oil. Permit to marinate for 1 hour.
2.   While the pork marinates, set your Anova unit to 165F/73.8C and permit the water shower to come to the right temperature. When the pork is marinated, place pork and flavors in a vacuum-fixed bag.
3.   Place the pack in the water shower for no less than one hour and up to four hours.
4.   When the pork is almost completed the process of cooking, heat a skillet or wok with one tablespoon of grapeseed or vegetable oil until hot. Throw in the water chestnuts, scallions, clam sauce and cilantro and sauté for around three minutes.
5.   Open the vacuum-fixed pack and mix in the pork and flavors and eliminate from heat.
6.   Divide the lettuce leaves and spoon in the pork blend to serve.

Nutritional Info: Calories: 97, Sodium: 156mg, Dietary Fiber: 0.5g, Total Fat: 3g, Total Carbs: 8.8g, Protein: 8g.

Sous Vide Wagyu Meatballs

SERVINGS: 6 | PREP TIME: 20 MINUTES | COOK TIME: 1-4 HOURS

Wagyu is one of the most wanton cuts of meat accessible and your sous vide makes certain to seal in the juices in general and flavor it brings to the table. This formula will show you a few astonishing flavors that will make your wagyu much more spectacular.

INGREDIENTS:

1 pound wagyu or ground hamburger 1/4 cup bread crumbs
3 ounces milk
1/2 teaspoon salt
1/4 teaspoon dark pepper 1 huge egg, beaten
1/2 shallot, stripped and diced
3 tablespoons cleaved new parsley
1 tablespoon dried oregano
1 tablespoon garlic powder

3 tablespoons ground parmesan
cheddar 2 tablespoons vegetable oil

INSTRUCTIONS:

1. In a bowl, blend the ground meat in with any remaining fixings. Don't over blend excessively or meatballs will become dense.
2. Form into balls that are around two crawls in diameter.
3. Put the meatballs onto a plate and freeze them for an hour.
4. Once firm, place the meatballs in a vacuum-fixed bag.
5. Set your Anova for 135F/57C and place pack into the water shower for something like one hour and not more than four hours.
6. Remove the meatballs from the water shower and serve.
7. Note: If you lean toward a crisper meatball basically wipe them off and warm two tablespoons of oil in a container. Sauté the meatballs for a considerable length of time or until browned.

Nutritional Info: Calories: 240, Sodium: 318mg, Dietary Fiber: 0.7g, Total Fat: 12g, Total Carbs: 6g, Protein: 26g.

Sous Vide Chinese Crispy Pork Belly

SERVINGS: 8 | PREP TIME: 10 MINUTES | COOK TIME: 6 HOURS

This tasty customary dish is beguilingly simple to get ready and your sous vide takes all of the mystery out of cooking amazing pork belly.

INGREDIENTS:

2 pounds pork midsection
(skin on) 2 steel or wood
skewers
2 teaspoons salt
1 teaspoon white pepper
1 teaspoon five flavor
powder 1 teaspoon white
pepper
3 tablespoons white vinegar

INSTRUCTIONS:

1. Set your Anova unit to 165F/73.8C.
2. In a little bowl, consolidate the salt, white pepper and Chinese five

zest power. Sprinkle half of the combination liberally to cover the pork midsection. Try not to utilize the flavors on the fat side.

3. Place your pork midsection in a vacuum-fixed bag.
4. Submerge the pork tummy in the water shower for somewhere around six and not over eight hours. At the point when the pork stomach is done cooking, eliminate from the water shower and eliminate from the bag.
5. Dry the pork gut totally and utilize the excess portion of the flavor blend to prepare the pork tummy again.
6. Set your oven to high and spot the pork midsection on a baking sheet.
7. Cook under the oven for ten to twelve minutes or until skin has reached wanted crispiness.
8. Remove from grill and cut into little pieces.

Nutritional Info: Calories: 523, Sodium: 1832mg, Dietary Fiber: 0.9g, Total Fat: 30.5g, Total Carbs: 0.6g, Protein: 53g.

CHAPTER 9
VEGETABLES

Agnolotti with Artichoke Sauce

SERVINGS: 4 | PREP TIME: 15 MINUTES | COOK TIME: 30

This formula is a simple method for making your pasta and sauce at the same time, and your Foodsaver will make putting away extras truly basic. On the off chance that you can't observe Agnolotti you can simply utilize ravioli instead.

INGREDIENTS:

For Sauce:
1 (9-ounce) bundle frozen artichoke hearts, defrosted and coarsely hacked 1 cup frozen peas (don't thaw)
1 cup half-and-half
1 clove garlic, smashed
1/8 teaspoon red pepper flakes
1 teaspoon finely ground lemon
zing 2 teaspoons new lemon juice
Salt

For Pasta:
1 pound refrigerated cheddar agnolotti (or
ravioli) 1 cup ground parmesan cheese
1/4 cup new basil leaves, chopped

INSTRUCTIONS:

For Sauce:
1. Combine the artichokes, cream, garlic, red pepper chips and 1/4 teaspoon salt in a vacuum-fixed bag.
2. Set your Anova to 165F/73.8C and put the pack in the water shower for 30 minutes.

For Pasta:
3. While the sauce is cooking, heat a pot of water to the point of boiling and add the agnolotti. Channel the pasta yet hold 1/2 of the pasta water.
4. Heat a dish over medium hotness, and when the sauce is done in the Anova, eliminate the pack from the water and empty the substance into the skillet. Add the pasta and 1/2 cup of pasta water and mix to cover. Then, at that point, add the parmesan cheddar and mix. Serve finished off with the cleaved basil.

Nutritional Info: Calories: 525, Sodium: 1214mg, Dietary Fiber: 7g, Total Fat: 27.6g, Total Carbs: 36g, Protein: 475g.

Sous Vide Glazed Baby Carrots

SERVINGS: 6 | PREP TIME: 10 MINUTES | COOK TIME: 1 HOUR 10 MINUTES

Cooking carrots sous vide is fast and simple, but since the carrots are cooking in their own juices, they hold so much flavor.

INGREDIENTS:

1 pound child entire child
carrots 2 tablespoons unsalted
butter
1 tablespoon granulated
sugar Salt
Freshly ground dark pepper

INSTRUCTIONS:

1. Set your Anova to 183F/83.8C.
2. In a vacuum-fixed pack, join the carrots, spread, sugar, and 1/2 teaspoon of salt and seal.
3. Submerge the sack in the water shower for one hour.
4. When the carrots are practically gotten done, heat a dish over high heat.
5. Empty the carrots into the container and cook until the fluid from the pack thickens and turns into a glaze.

Nutritional Info: Calories: 68, Sodium: 86mg, Dietary Fiber: 2.2g, Total Fat: 3.9g, Total Carbs: 8.2g, Protein: 0.5g.

Frittata with Asparagus, Tomato, and Fontina

SERVINGS: 3 | PREP TIME: 10 MINUTES | COOK TIME: 1 HOUR

We've as of now talked about how the sous vide is ideal for cooking eggs to the ideal consistency, and this formula will help you how to make a frittata that will make any morning meal special.

INGREDIENTS:

6 enormous eggs
2 tablespoons whipping cream
1/4 teaspoon newly ground dark pepper
1 tablespoon olive oil
1 tablespoon butter
12 ounces asparagus, managed, cut into 1/4 to 1/2-inch
pieces 1 tomato, cultivated, diced
2 teaspoons salt
3 ounces fontina, diced

INSTRUCTIONS:

1. Heat your Anova to 176F/80C.
2. While the water is coming up to temperature, heat a skillet over medium hotness adding the olive oil.
3. At the point when oil is hot, add the asparagus, salt, pepper, and tomato. Sauté until the asparagus is delicate and eliminate from heat.
4. Beat the eggs and fill a vacuum-fixed pack. Add the substance of the dish alongside the spread and diced fontina. Lower the sack into the water and attempt to keep it level on the lower part of the container.
5. Cook for one hour and eliminate from the water shower. Cut the sack open and serve.

Nutritional Info: Calories: 383, Sodium: 2339mg, Dietary Fiber: 2.7g, Total Fat: 31g, Total Carbs: 7g, Protein: 23g.

Curried Potatoes and Chickpeas

SERVINGS: 8 | PREP TIME: 20 MINUTES | COOK TIME: 2 HOURS

This basic yet tasty dish works out positively for various proteins and is not difficult to make yet packs complicated and extraordinary flavors.

INGREDIENTS:

1-1/2 pounds Yukon gold potatoes, stripped and cut into 3/4-inch
pieces 3 tablespoons unsalted butter
1-1/2 teaspoons curry
powder 1/4 teaspoon
cayenne pepper
1 (15-ounce) can chickpeas, depleted and

flushed 2 cups singed onions
1/2 cup plain Greek yogurt
1/4 cup slashed new cilantro, in addition to leaves
for garnish 2 tablespoons new lime juice
1 jalapeno pepper, daintily
cut Salt

INSTRUCTIONS:

1. Set your Anova to 200F/93.3C. While the water is warming, heat 2 tablespoons of margarine in a pan and fry the onions.
2. Add the cut potatoes, curry powder, cayenne pepper, chickpeas, and onions to a vacuum-fixed bag.
3. Submerge the pack in the water shower and cook for something like two hours and not more than four.
4. In a little bowl, join the yogurt, cilantro, and lime juice. Eliminate the pack from the water shower and split between little dishes. Top with the yogurt sauce and cut jalapenos to serve.

Nutritional Info: Calories: 322, Sodium: 84mg, Dietary Fiber: 11.3g, Total Fat: 7.9g, Total Carbs: 52.2g, Protein: 13.3g.

Sous Vide Mixed Vegetables

SERVINGS: 6 | PREP TIME: 15 MINUTES | COOK TIME: 60-90 MINUTES

Sous vide is an astounding approach to making delightful vegetable dishes. Go ahead and try different things with whatever is in season.

INGREDIENTS:

1-1/2 pounds blended vegetables like yellow squash, zucchini, red and green peppers, eggplant)
2 tablespoons olive oil
2 tablespoons new spices finely cleaved (parsley, thyme and chives) Salt and pepper, to taste

INSTRUCTIONS:

1. Heat your Anova shower to 183F/83C.
2. Wash, strip, and cut the vegetables into 1-inch pieces. Put every one of the vegetables into a vacuum-fixed sack. Add the oil, spices

and salt and pepper to the pack before vacuum sealing.
3. Place the sacks in the water and cook for around 60-90 minutes.
4. Once cooked, serve quickly or cool the vegetables and utilize later. You can utilize them to make the accompanying delightful plans: Couscous with Mediterranean Vegetables, Vegetable Flatbread Wraps, or Hearty Vegetable Soup.

Nutritional Info: Calories: 81, Sodium: 255mg, Dietary Fiber: 4.3g, Total Fat: 5.0g, Total Carbs: 8.2g, Protein: 1.7g.

Sous Vide Summer Salsa

SERVINGS: 10 | PREP TIME: 10 MINUTES | COOK TIME: 30 MINUTES

Salsa isn't normally cooked however utilizing the low even hotness of the sous vide to mix the flavors will add another aspect to your salsa.

INGREDIENTS:

2 jars of sweet corn (yellow or white) 1 can dark beans
1/2 red onion, chopped
1 red ringer pepper,
hacked 1/2 cup sugar
1/2 cup rice wine vinegar (red wine or champagne vinegar will likewise work) Salt

INSTRUCTIONS:

1. Set your Anova to 125F/51.6C and join every one of the fixings in a vacuum-fixed bag.
2. Seal the sack and lower in the water shower for 30 minutes.
3. Remove pack from water and chill in the cooler for one hour before serving.

Nutritional Info: Calories: 155, Sodium: 2mg, Dietary Fiber: 4.4g, Total Fat: 0.6g, Total Carbs: 32.3g, Protein: 5.6g.

Sous Vide Balsamic Beets

SERVINGS: 6 | PREP TIME: 10 MINUTES | COOK TIME: 2 HOURS

Using your Anova is a brilliant method for imbuing the kind of balsamic vinegar into beets for a flavor stuffed vegetable dish.

INGREDIENTS:

6 medium beets (2 bundles, or around 3-1/2
pounds) 1 teaspoon salt
2 tablespoons additional virgin
olive oil 1/3 cup cheap balsamic
vinegar 1 tablespoon maple syrup
Freshly ground dark pepper, to taste

INSTRUCTIONS:

1. Set your Anova to 185F/85C.
2. Place the slashed beets, olive oil, salt and two tablespoons of balsamic vinegar into a vacuum-fixed bag.
3. Submerge the sack in the water shower and cook for 2 hours.
4. While the beets are cooking, consolidate the leftover balsamic vinegar, and maple syrup in a little saucepan.
5. Heat on medium until the blend has diminished marginally, causing sure not to consume the vinegar.
6. Remove the beets from the water shower and move to a medium bowl. Pour balsamic decrease over the beets and mix to coat.

Nutritional Info: Calories: 74, Sodium: 427mg, Dietary Fiber: 1g, Total Fat: 4.8g, Total Carbs: 7.3g, Protein: 0.8g.

Spicy Butter Poached Asparagus

SERVINGS: 4 | PREP TIME: 10 MINUTES | COOK TIME: 10-12 MINUTES

Add a kick to conventional asparagus for delectable outcomes. Utilizing your Anova to make vegetables gives you unlimited oversight over surface and flavor.

INGREDIENTS:

1 pack of asparagus,
managed 3 tablespoons
unsalted spread 1/2 teaspoon

cayenne pepper Pinch of salt

INSTRUCTIONS:

1. Set your Anova for 185F/85C.
2. Trim the bottoms of the asparagus and spot them level in a vacuum-fixed bag.
3. Melt the margarine and add the cayenne pepper. Shower the flavored margarine over the asparagus and utilize a vacuum sealer to seal the bag.
4. When the water shower has arrived at the legitimate temperature place the sack in the water and cook for 10 to 12 minutes.
5. Remove the pack from the water and sprinkle a touch of salt on the asparagus before serving.

Nutritional Info: Calories: 78, Sodium: 61mg, Dietary Fiber: 0g, Total Fat: 9g, Total Carbs: 0.3g, Protein: 0.2g.

Sous Vide Root Vegetables with Brown Butter

SERVINGS: 6 | PREP TIME: 30 MINUTES | COOK TIME: 3 HOURS

Root vegetables are an appetizing side and cooking them sous vide will add significantly more gritty flavor.

INGREDIENTS:

1 turnip, stripped and cut into pieces
8 child carrots, stripped and cut into pieces
1 medium parsnip, stripped and cut into pieces
1/2 medium red onion, stripped and cut into
pieces 4 cloves garlic, crushed
4 branches new rosemary, on the
stem 2 tablespoons extra-virgin
olive oil 2 tablespoons butter
Salt and newly ground pepper

INSTRUCTIONS:

1. Set your Anova to 185F/85C.
2. Combine all fixings in an enormous vacuum-fixed bag.

3. Submerge the pack in the water shower and cook for 3 hours.
4. Remove the pack from the water shower and strain out the cooking liquid.
5. Heat a pan over medium hotness and add the cooking fluid, lessening until it somewhat thickens.
6. Pour the fluid over the vegetables to serve.

Nutritional Info: Calories: 114, Sodium: 55mg, Dietary Fiber: 2.9g, Total Fat: 8.9g, Total Carbs: 9.2g, Protein: 0.9g.

Sous Vide Butternut Squash

SERVINGS: 4 | PRE TIME: 10 MINUTES | COOK TIME: 1 HOUR

Butternut squash is loaded with generous flavors that are just upgraded with sous vide cooking.

INGREDIENTS:

1 butternut squash, stripped and cut into pieces 1 tablespoon butter
1 twig new thyme
1 twig new sage
1 teaspoon salt
1 tablespoon light brown sugar

INSTRUCTIONS:

1. Set your Anova to 155F/68C.
2. Place the diced squash, spread, spices, and salt in a huge vacuum-fixed bag.
3. Submerge in the water shower for 1 hour.
4. Remove from water shower and spot on a baking sheet. Heat your stove to 400F.
5. Sprinkle the earthy colored sugar over the squash and cook in the broiler for 10 minutes.

Nutritional Info: Calories: 53, Sodium: 604mg, Dietary Fiber: 1.1g, Total Fat: 3.0g, Total Carbs: 6.9g, Protein: 0.5g.

Sous Vide Maple Glazed Sweet Potatoes

SERVINGS: 6 | PREP TIME: 10 MINUTES | COOK TIME: 60-90 MINUTES

Your Anova is a superb method for cooking yams and lock in all of their scrumptious flavor.

INGREDIENTS:

2-1/2 pounds yams, stripped and cut into 1-1/2-inch pieces 1/3
cup unadulterated maple syrup
2 tablespoons spread,
liquefied 1 tablespoon
lemon juice 1/2 teaspoon
salt

INSTRUCTIONS:

1. Set your Anova to 190F/87.7C.
2. Combine every one of the fixings in a vacuum-fixed bag.
3. Submerge the sack in the water shower and cook for somewhere
   around an hour and not longer than 90 minutes.
4. Remove from sack and sprinkle the fluid over the potatoes to serve.

Nutritional Info: Calories: 303, Sodium: 240mg, Dietary Fiber: 7.8g, Total
Fat: 4.2g, Total Carbs: 64.5g, Protein: 3.0g.

CHAPTER 10
CHICKEN

Sous Vide Bourbon Chicken

SERVINGS: 4 | PREP TIME: 20 MINUTES | COOK TIME: 1 HOUR 10 MINUTES

This is a very simple formula that loads a huge load of flavor with barely any work, and it doesn't need any whiskey. It was initially made by a Chinese cook dealing with Bourbon Street in New Orleans.

INGREDIENTS:

2 pounds boneless chicken bosoms, cut into scaled down
pieces 2 tablespoons olive oil
1 garlic clove,
squashed 1/4
teaspoon ginger
3/4 teaspoons squashed red pepper
chips 1/4 cup apple juice
1/3 cup light earthy
colored sugar 2
tablespoons ketchup
1 tablespoon juice
vinegar 1/2 cup water
1/3 cup soy sauce

INSTRUCTIONS:

1. Set your Anova to 150F/65.5C.
2. In a medium container, heat the oil until hot however not smoking. Add the chicken and cook just until marginally seared. Eliminate chicken from heat.
3. Add the leftover fixings and chicken to a vacuum-fixed bag.
4. Place the pack into the water shower and cook for 60 minutes. This will give the fixings time to consolidate into a tasty sauce and wrap up cooking the chicken.
5. Remove the pack from the water shower and present with steamed white or earthy colored rice, or your selection of sous vide vegetables that can be cooked in a different sack at the equivalent time.

Nutritional Info: Calories: 566, Sodium: 1482mg, Dietary Fiber: 0g, Total

Sous Vide Chicken Teriyaki

SERVINGS: 6 | PREP TIME: 10 MINUTES | COOK TIME: 1 HOUR

Your sous vide is an extraordinary method for making this Japanese top pick at home without all the abundance oil that eateries normally use.

INGREDIENTS:

1 tablespoon cornstarch 1 tablespoon cold water
1/2 cup white sugar
1/2 cup soy sauce
1/4 cup juice
vinegar
1 clove garlic, minced
1/2 teaspoon ground ginger
1/4 teaspoon ground dark pepper 12 skinless chicken thighs

INSTRUCTIONS:

1. Set your Anova to 165F/73.8C.
2. In a little bowl, join the cornstarch, cold water, sugar, soy sauce, vinegar, garlic, ginger and ground dark pepper.
3. Add sauce blend and chicken thighs to a vacuum-fixed bag.
4. When the water shower has arrived at the right temperature, lower the pack and cook for 1 hour.
5. Heat grill to high.
6. Remove the pack from the shower and spot chicken on a baking sheet and brush with sauce from the sack. Cook the chicken for 2 to 3 minutes on each side under the oven to sear.
7. Serve with steamed white or earthy colored rice, or sous vide vegetables.

Fat: 6.2g, Total Carbs: 19.9g, Protein: 25.5g.

Sous Vide Barbecue Chicken

SERVINGS: 4 | PREP TIME: 10 MINUTES | COOK TIME: 1-1/2 HOURS

For the most delicious chicken bosoms, sous vide is the house cook's closest companion. Never again stress that your chicken bosoms will be overcooked and tough.

INGREDIENTS:

4 chicken breasts
1 or 2 twigs of new thyme
1 or 2 branches of new rosemary
1/2 teaspoon ancho pepper, or other stew
powder BBQ Sauce

INSTRUCTIONS:

1. Set your Anova for 141F/60C.
2. Season the chicken with salt and pepper and spot them in a vacuum-fixed bag.
3. Add the rosemary and thyme to the sack and seal.
4. Place the pack in the water shower and cook for somewhere around 1-1/2 hours and not more than 2-1/2.
5. When the chicken is nearly completed the process of cooking heat either your barbecue or oven to high. Eliminate the chicken from the pack and wipe off with paper towels.
6. Slather with BBQ sauce and spot them on the barbecue or under the oven for sufficiently long to roast the sauce. Serve immediately.

Nutritional Info: Calories: 123, Sodium: 62mg, Dietary Fiber: 0g, Total Fat: 4.8g, Total Carbs: 0.9g, Protein: 18.1g.

Sous Vide Tequila Lime Chicken

SERVINGS: 4 | PREP TIME: 20 MINUTES | COOK TIME: 1 HOUR

Getting a few roast on chicken bosoms can add a ton of flavor however cooking bosoms on the barbecue can likewise wind up drying out the meat.

Utilizing your Anova and oven, you can get all the kind of the barbecue and still end up with succulent delicate meat.

INGREDIENTS:

3 tablespoons olive
oil 3 tablespoons
tequila
1 tablespoon lime zing, from around 2
limes 4 cloves garlic, minced
1-1/4 teaspoons ancho bean stew
powder 1/2 teaspoon ground
coriander
1/4 teaspoon dried
oregano 1-1/4 teaspoons
salt
1/2 teaspoon newly ground dark pepper
2 teaspoons honey
4 boneless skinless chicken breasts
1 lime, cut into wedges, for serving

INSTRUCTIONS:

1. Set your Anova for 150F/65.5C.
2. Season the chicken with salt and pepper and set aside.
3. Combine each of different fixings in a bowl and stir.
4. Place the chicken bosoms in a vacuum-fixed sack, add 2/3 of the flavoring blend, and seal. The vacuum-fixed pack will marinate the meat as it cooks.
5. Place in the water shower and cook for something like 1 hour and not more than 2.
6. When you are nearly completed the process of cooking, heat your kettle to high.
7. Remove the chicken from the sack and wipe off with paper towels.
8. Place on a baking sheet and treat with the leftover flavoring mixture.
9. Cook under the grill for sufficiently long for the chicken to burn. Flip the chicken over and singe that side.
10. Serve right away. This dish works out positively for a new corn salad.

Nutritional Info: Calories: 131, Sodium: 775mg, Dietary Fiber: 1.1g, Total Fat: 3.4g, Total Carbs: 6.6g, Protein: 12.8g.

Super Healthy Sous Vide Chicken Parmesan

SERVINGS: 4 | PREP TIME: 15 MINUTES | COOK TIME: 1 HOUR

Chicken parmesan is normally singed, and that absorbs a ton of oil, yet this straightforward formula will tell you the best way to get all of the kind of exemplary chicken parmesan without stressing over extra calories.

INGREDIENTS:

4 boneless, skinless chicken breasts
1/2 pound low dampness, entire milk mozzarella
1 28-ounce can entire, stripped tomatoes (ideally San Marzano) 3 cloves garlic, crushed
1 tablespoon new or dry oregano
1 tablespoon new hacked or dry basil

1 tablespoon extra-virgin olive oil
1 tablespoon lemon
juice 2 teaspoons salt
Pinch of ground pepper
1 bundle spaghetti or linguini (for serving)
Grated parmesan (for serving)

INSTRUCTIONS:

1. Set your Anova to 150F/65.5C.
2. Season the chicken bosoms with 1 teaspoon of salt and a touch of dark pepper.
3. Place the chicken in a vacuum-fixed pack and cook the chicken in the water shower for something like 1 hour and not more than 2.
4. While the chicken is cooking, make the sauce.
5. In a food processor or blender, add the tomatoes, garlic, oregano, basil, and the leftover salt and pepper. Beat a few times until the tomatoes are hacked yet not exactly smooth.
6. Pour the substance of the food processor into a medium pan and add the olive oil.
7. Heat over medium hotness, mixing habitually. At the point when the sauce has obscured a piece add the lemon squeeze and eliminate from heat. This should take around 20 minutes.
8. Heat a pot of salted water on the oven. When bubbling, add the spaghetti or linguini, cooking in view of bundle bearings, and drain.
9. Slice the mozzarella into 1/4-thick rounds.
10. Remove the chicken from the sack and wipe off with paper towels.
11. Arrange the chicken on a baking sheet and spot the cut mozzarella on top. Heat grill to high and spot the baking sheet in the oven, cooking until the cheddar is beginning to liquefy and brown.
12. Remove chicken from oven. Organize pasta on plates and spot chicken on the pasta.
13. To serve, top the chicken bosoms with a liberal measure of pureed tomatoes, and ground parmesan cheese.

Nutritional Info: Calories: 383, Sodium: 93mg, Dietary Fiber: 1.1g, Total Fat: 11g, Total Carbs: 46.1g, Protein: 25.4g.

Sous Vide Crispy Drumsticks

SERVINGS: 6 | PREP TIME: 10 MINUTES | COOK TIME: 1 HOUR

These drumsticks are soggy and delicious within because of your Anova's even heat.

INGREDIENTS:

12 drumsticks
6 tablespoons vegetable
oil Salt
Pepper

INSTRUCTIONS:

1. Set your Anova to 158F/70C.
2. Season the drumsticks with salt and pepper and seal 4 in each vacuum-fixed bag.
3. Submerge the sacks in the water shower and cook for one hour.
4. When the chicken is almost completed the process of cooking, heat an enormous skillet with the oil over medium-high heat.
5. Remove the chicken from the packs and cook rapidly in the skillet until skin is fresh and brilliant brown.

Nutritional Info: Calories: 276, Sodium: 101mg, Dietary Fiber: 0g, Total Fat: 18.9g, Total Carbs: 0.1g, Protein: 25.3g.

Sous Vide Turkey Leg

SERVINGS: 2 | PREP TIME: 10 MINUTES | COOK TIME: 6-7 HOURS

A top pick at the area reasonable, turkey legs are not difficult to make at home utilizing your Anova, and you're ensured to have the most delicate meat possible.

INGREDIENTS:

2 huge turkey legs, around 1 pound
every 3 tablespoons butter
4 huge new sage leaves, folded by hand 1
huge branch of rosemary
2 garlic cloves, crushed and
stripped 1/2 teaspoon salt
1/2 teaspoon newly ground dark pepper

INSTRUCTIONS:

1. Set your Anova to 170F/77C.
2. Place turkey legs into a vacuum-fixed pack with the margarine, sage, rosemary, garlic, salt and pepper, and seal.
3. Place the pack in the water shower and cook for 6 to 7 hours.
4. Remove the pack from the water shower and pour the liquefied spread from the sack into a bowl.
5. Discard the pack and any remaining contents.
6. Pour the spread into a huge skillet and hotness to high.
7. Sear the turkey legs until they are brown on all sides.

Nutritional Info: Calories: 951, Sodium: 1024mg, Dietary Fiber: 2.9g, Total Fat: 40.9g, Total Carbs: 5.4g, Protein: 133.8g.

Brown Sugar-Garlic Chicken

SERVINGS: 2 | PREP TIME: 10 MINUTES | COOK TIME: 1 HOUR

This basic formula is a pleasant curve on chicken bosom that adds heaps of intriguing flavor.

INGREDIENTS:

4 teaspoons brown sugar
12 ounces boneless, skinless chicken
bosoms 1 clove garlic
2 tablespoons
spread Dash dark
pepper

INSTRUCTIONS:

1. Set your Anova for 150F/65.5C.
2. In a little sauce dish, soften the spread and add brown the clove of garlic.
3. Place the chicken in a vacuum-fixed pack and add the garlic margarine just as the dark pepper and seal.
4. Place the sack in the water shower and cook for something like 1 hour and not more than 2.
5. When you are nearly wrapped up cooking the chicken, heat your oven to high.
6. Remove the chicken from the pack and spot on a baking sheet.

7. Sprinkle the earthy colored sugar over the chicken and cook under the oven for one little while so the sugar dissolves and makes a coating on the chicken. This is brilliant presented with steamed rice or vegetables.

Nutritional Info: Calories: 450, Sodium: 230mg, Dietary Fiber: 0g, Total Fat: 24.1g, Total Carbs: 6.4g, Protein: 49.4g.

Sous Vide Spicy Chicken Sliders

SERVINGS: 8 | PREP TIME: 20 MINUTES | COOK TIME: 1 HOUR

These sliders are a great method for pressing heaps of flavor into a simple to eat sandwich.

INGREDIENTS:

1 pound ground
chicken Salt
Ground pepper
1 tablespoon cayenne pepper
1 tablespoon ground mustard
seed 1 teaspoon dried oregano
1/3 cup bread crumbs
1 tablespoon vegetable
oil 12 delicate slider
buns
Butter lettuce, for serving

INSTRUCTIONS:

1. Set your Anova for 150F/65.5C.
2. In an enormous bowl, join the chicken, salt, pepper, mustard, cayenne pepper, oregano, and bread pieces. Blend well and make little patties.
3. Place the patties in a solitary layer in a vacuum-fixed bag.
4. Submerge in the water shower and cook for 1 hour.
5. When the chicken is nearly completed the process of cooking, heat an enormous skillet with the oil over medium heat.
6. Sear every patty for 1 moment for each side and serve on the slider buns finished off with lettuce.

Nutritional Info: Calories: 218, Sodium: 224mg, Dietary Fiber: 1.4g, Total

Sous Vide Vietnamese Chicken Wings

SERVINGS: 6 | PREP TIME: 10 MINUTES | COOK TIME: 1 HOUR

These wings are not difficult to make and loaded with flavor. Cooking them sous vide rather than on the barbecue will guarantee that they stay soggy and juicy.

INGREDIENTS:

4 cloves minced garlic 1/4 cup lime juice
1/4 cup fish sauce
2 tablespoons soy sauce
3 tablespoons earthy colored sugar 2 tablespoons vegetable oil
2 pounds chicken wings
Sprig of cilantro (for serving)
3 tablespoons cut chilies (for serving)

INSTRUCTIONS:

1. Set your Anova for 170F/76.6C.
2. In a little bowl, join all fixings with the exception of the chicken wings.
3. Place the wings in a vacuum-sealed bag, pour in the marinade, and seal. For extra flavorful wings, place the bag in the refrigerator for a few hours.
4. Submerge the bag in the water bath and cook for at least 1 hour and up to 4 hours. When you are almost finished cooking, heat your broiler to high.
5. Remove the wings from the bag and discard the cooking liquid.
6. Place the wings on a baking sheet and cook under the broiler for a few minutes to slightly char the wings.
7. To serve, garnish with cilantro and sliced chilies.

Fat: 16.2g, Total Carbs: 8.8g, Protein: 44.8g.

Sous Vide Crispy Chicken Thighs

SERVINGS: 6 | PREP TIME: 5 MINUTES | COOK TIME: 1 HOUR

These are without a doubt; the most tender chicken thighs you've ever had. The crispy skin is just the icing on the cake.

INGREDIENTS:

6 boneless, skin-on chicken thighs
Salt and freshly ground pepper, to taste
2 garlic cloves, lightly smashed with a
knife 2 or 3 fresh thyme sprigs
2 tablespoons unsalted butter
2 tablespoons canola oil, plus more as needed

INSTRUCTIONS:

1. Set your Anova for 150F/65.5C.
2. Season the meat side of the chicken thighs with salt and pepper, then seal in vacuum-sealed bag.
3. Place the bag into the water bath and cook for at least 1 hour and not more that 2 hours.
4. When finished cooking, remove the chicken from the bag and place on a baking sheet. Place the baking sheet in the refrigerator for one hour.
5. Just before you're ready to serve, remove the chicken from the refrigerator and dry with paper towels.
6. Heat 2 tablespoon of oil in a medium skillet and cook the thighs skin side down until crisp. This should take about 8 minutes.
7. Remove from the pan and serve immediately to maintain crispy skin. Do not cover or the skin will become soggy.

Nutritional Info: Calories: 157, Sodium: 64mg, Dietary Fiber: 0g, Total Fat: 11.6g, Total Carbs: 0.7g, Protein: 12.2g.

Sous Vide Chicken with Sun Dried Tomato Vinaigrette

SERVINGS: 4 | PREP TIME: 15 MINUTES | COOK TIME: 90 MINUTES

This easy to make chicken dish is packed with complex flavors and just the right amount of heat to keep things exciting.

INGREDIENTS:

4 skin-on chicken breasts,
Salt and fresh ground black
pepper 1 poblano pepper
1/2 cup oil-packed sun-dried tomatoes, drained and
chopped 2 tablespoons of oil from tomatoes
1 teaspoon honey
1/2 teaspoon soy
sauce 2 teaspoons
lemon juice
1 medium shallot,
minced 1 tablespoon
vegetable oil

INSTRUCTIONS:

1. Set your Anova to 150F/65C.
2. Season the chicken breasts with salt and pepper in a vacuum-sealed bag.
3. In another vacuum-sealed bag combine the poblano, sun-dried tomatoes, oil, honey, soy sauce, lemon juice, and shallot.
4. Submerge both bags in the water bath and cook for 90 minutes.
5. When almost finished cooking, heat a medium skillet over medium heat and add the vegetable oil.
6. Remove chicken from the vacuum-sealed bag and sear, skin side down until skin is crispy.
7. Divide the chicken onto plates and top with warm tomato mixture.

Nutritional Info: Calories: 197, Sodium: 80mg, Dietary Fiber: 0.8g, Total Fat:

13.7g, Total Carbs: 5.1g, Protein: 13.8g.

Sous Vide Chicken and Dumplings

SERVINGS: 4 | PREP TIME: 15 MINUTES | COOK TIME: 1-1/2

This traditional country style recipe can also be made in a slow cooker, but for faster results use your Anova.

INGREDIENTS:

4 skinless boneless chicken
breasts 2 tablespoons butter
1 onion, diced
2 packages of refrigerated biscuit
dough 2 cans of cream of chicken
soup

INSTRUCTIONS:

1. Set your Anova to 155F/68.3C.
2. Place the chicken, butter, onion, and soup in a vacuum-sealed bag.
3. Submerge the bag in the water bath and cook for 2 hours.
4. When the bag containing the chicken has cooked for 1-1/2 hours, tear the biscuit dough into small pieces and place in a different vacuum- sealed bag.
5. Submerge the bag with the biscuit dough in the water bath and cook for 30 minutes.
6. Remove both bags at the same time, combine and serve.

Nutritional Info: Calories: 346, Sodium: 1263mg, Dietary Fiber: 0.8g, Total Fat: 20.7g, Total Carbs: 22g, Protein: 17.7g.

Sous Vide Chicken Liver Mousse

SERVINGS: 6 | PREP TIME: 20 MINUTES | COOK TIME: 90 MINUTES

The secret to amazing mousse is keeping the livers from overcooking. Luckily, your sous vide takes all of the guess work out of maintaining an even temperature.

INGREDIENTS:

3 shallots, minced
2 sprigs fresh
thyme 8 ounces

cognac
1 pound chicken
livers 4 large eggs
1/4 cup heavy
cream 2 teaspoons
salt

INSTRUCTIONS:

1. Set your Anova to 155F/68C.
2. In a large pan over medium heat, combine the shallots, and thyme, and cook until the shallots are beginning to caramelize. Remove from heat.
3. In a food processor, combine the cognac, chicken livers, eggs, and heavy cream, and blend until smooth.
4. Then add the shallots and thyme and pulse the food processor several times.
5. Place the mixture in a vacuum-sealed bag and submerge in the water bath for 90 minutes.
6. Remove from the water bath and place in the refrigerator for 1 hour to cool before serving.

Nutritional Info: Calories: 282, Sodium: 883mg, Dietary Fiber: 0g, Total Fat: 10.2g, Total Carbs: 2.8g, Protein: 23g.

Sous Vide Spinach and Rice Stuffed Trout

SERVINGS: 2 | PREP TIME: 15 MINUTES | COOK TIME: 45 MINUTES

Whole trout are tasty and delicate, and this recipe will teach you how to make an entire meal with just your Anova.

INGREDIENTS:

2 whole trout, heads and tails removed 1/2 cup white parboiled rice
1/2 pound spinach, chopped
1 tablespoon garlic, finely chopped 1 teaspoon onion powder
2 tablespoons butter, melted Salt & pepper to taste

INSTRUCTIONS:

1. Set your Anova to 130F/54.4C.
2. In a large bowl, combine the rice, spinach, garlic, onion powder and butter. Stir well.
3. Salt and pepper the insides of the trout and then stuff with the rice and spinach mixture.
4. Place the stuffed trout in separate vacuum-sealed bags. Because your Vacuum sealer creates a perfect seal it will keep the stuffing inside the fish as it cooks.
5. Submerge the bags in the water and cook for 45 minutes.
6. Remove the bags from the water and serve the fish with the stuffing still inside.

Nutritional Info: Calories: 426, Sodium: 294mg, Dietary Fiber: 3.4g, Total

Fat: 17.6g, Total Carbs: 43.8g, Protein: 23.6g.

Sous Vide Black Cod Filets

SERVINGS: 2 | PREP TIME: 15 MINUTES | COOK TIME: 20 MINUTES

Black cod is the fattiest and most tender of all cods, and cooking it sous vide guarantees perfect texture.

INGREDIENTS:

1 pound of black cod fillets, skin-on and scaled 3 tablespoons butter
3 sprigs of
thyme 3
tablespoons salt
1 cup of water
Lemon wedges

INSTRUCTIONS:

1. Set your Anova to 125F/51.6C.
2. In a large bowl, combine the water, salt and cod filets. Allow them to brine for 10 minutes, then rise the fish thoroughly with cold water.
3. Place the filets in separate vacuum-sealed bags with 1 tablespoon butter and one sprig of thyme per bag.
4. Seal the bags and place in the water bath for 20 minutes.
5. When the fish is nearly cooked, heat your broiler to low.
6. Remove the fish from the bags and place on a backing rack, skin side up, and broil for 5 minutes, or until the skin is crispy.
7. Serve immediately to preserve crispy skin.

Nutritional Info: Calories: 404, Sodium: 306mg, Dietary Fiber: 1.7g, Total Fat: 19.6g, Total Carbs: 2.9g, Protein: 52.4g.

Sous Vide Scrambled Eggs with Smoked Salmon

SERVINGS: 3 | PREP TIME: 15 MINUTES | COOK TIME: 30

Eggs and salmon go together wonderfully, and your Anova can cook scrambled eggs to perfection.

INGREDIENTS:

6 large eggs
2 tablespoons fresh chives,
chopped 1/2 pound thin sliced
smoked salmon 1/2 cup crème
fraiche or sour cream 4 cups baby
spinach or arugula
3 tablespoons extra virgin olive
oil 2 tablespoons champagne
vinegar Salt
Black pepper

INSTRUCTIONS:

1. Set your Anova to 165F/73C.
2. In a bowl, whisk eggs together until smooth. Add the salt and pepper.
3. Pour eggs into a vacuum-sealed bag.
4. Place the bag into the water bath and set a timer for 10 minutes. When the timer goes off, remove the bag from the water and massage the bag to break up the eggs.
5. Place the bag back in the water bath and cook for another 10 minutes. Remove the bag and massage again before placing the bag back in the water bath for a final 10 minutes.
6. Remove the bag from the water, massage once more and divide the eggs on plates.
7. To make the salad, combine the olive oil and vinegar with a pinch of pepper and toss with the greens.
8. Top the eggs with chopped chives and slices of salmon. Then top the salmon with a dollop of crème fraiche and serve.

Nutritional Info: Calories: 461, Sodium: 227mg, Dietary Fiber: 1.4g, Total Fat: 36.9g, Total Carbs: 5.1g, Protein: 29.9g.

Sous Vide Parmesan Tilapia

Tilapia is a sweet and delicate whitefish that is easy to overcook with traditional methods. This recipe will show you how to make perfectly flaky fish with a flavorful topping.

INGREDIENTS:

1/2 cup parmesan
cheese 1/4 cup butter,
softened
3 tablespoons mayonnaise
2 tablespoons fresh lemon
juice 1/4 teaspoon dried basil
1/4 teaspoon ground black
pepper 1/8 teaspoon onion
powder
1/8 teaspoon celery
salt 2 pounds tilapia
fillets 2 tablespoons
olive oil

INSTRUCTIONS:

1. Set your Anova to 132F/55.5C.
2. Place Tilapia filets in a vacuum-sealed bag with the olive oil, seal and submerge in the water bath for 20 minutes.
3. In a small bowl, mix together the Parmesan cheese, butter, mayonnaise and lemon juice.
4. Season with dried basil, pepper, onion powder and celery salt. Mix and set aside.
5. When the tilapia is finished cooking, remove from the water bath and arrange filets on a baking sheet.
6. Heat your broiler to high and top the fish with the cheese mixture.
7. Cook under the broiler for just 2 or 3 minutes to brown the cheese and serve.

Nutritional Info: Calories: 394, Sodium: 242mg, Dietary Fiber: 0g, Total Fat:

....

24.3g, Total Carbs: 3.0g, Protein: 42.5g.

....

Sous Vide Mediterranean Halibut

SERVINGS: 2 | PREP TIME: 10 MINUTES | COOK TIME: 30 MINUTES

Halibut is a flaky yet meaty fish that needs to be cooked to the perfect temperature. Luckily, your Anova takes all the guess work out of perfectly cooked fish every time.

INGREDIENTS:

1 teaspoon extra-virgin olive oil 1 small onion, thinly sliced
2 tablespoons dry white wine 1 clove garlic, finely chopped 1 cup canned diced tomatoes
4 Kalamata olives, pitted and chopped 1/8 teaspoon dried oregano
1/8 teaspoon freshly grated orange zest 1/4 teaspoon salt, divided
1/4 teaspoon freshly ground pepper, divided 8 ounces thick-cut, Pacific Halibut filets

INSTRUCTIONS:

1. Set your Anova to 132F/55.5C.
2. Heat oil in a medium nonstick skillet over medium-high heat. Add onion and cook, stirring often, until lightly browned, 2 to 4 minutes.
3. Add wine and garlic and simmer for 30 seconds. Stir in tomatoes, olives, oregano and orange zest. Season with 1/8 teaspoon salt and 1/8 teaspoon pepper.
4. Season the halibut with salt and pepper and place the halibut in a vacuum-sealed bag. Submerge in the water bath for 30 minutes.
5. Remove the fish from the water bath and top with the tomato mixture. Serve with steamed white or brown rice, or sous vide vegetables.

Nutritional Info: Calories: 339, Sodium: 978mg, Dietary Fiber: 2.8g, Total

Sous Vide Salmon Croquettes

SERVINGS: 6 | PREP TIME: 20 MINUTES | COOK TIME: 20 MINUTES

Croquettes are an elegant and delicate way to prepare salmon, and your Anova makes achieving the perfect texture a breeze.

INGREDIENTS:

1 cup soft bread crumbs
1 tablespoon Dijon
mustard 1/4 teaspoon
pepper
8 medium green onions, finely
chopped 2 eggs, slightly beaten
1 pound salmon filet
2 tablespoons margarine or butter

INSTRUCTIONS:

1. Set your Anova to 125F/51.6C.
2. Place the salmon filet in a vacuum-sealed bag.
3. Submerge the bag in the water bath and cook for 15 to 20 minutes.
4. Remove the salmon from the bag and place in a large bowl. With a fork, shred the salmon into small pieces.
5. Combine all of the ingredients except for the butter with the salmon and mix thoroughly.
6. Heat a large skillet over medium heat and melt the butter.
7. Using large spoons, form the salmon mixture into balls or patties about 2 to 3 inches across.
8. When the butter is hot, place the patties into the pan and cook until just browned.
9. Remove from the pan and serve with fresh greens.
10. Tip: these croquettes can also be made into sandwiches. Simply serve each one on a slider bun for a delicious two-bite sandwich.

Nutritional Info: Calories: 179, Sodium: 171mg, Dietary Fiber: 0.8g, Total Fat: 10.2g, Total Carbs: 4.8g, Protein: 17.5g.

Sous Vide Salmon Steaks with Tarragon-Lemon Aioli

SERVINGS: 4 | PREP TIME: 30 MINUTES | COOK TIME: 1 HOUR

Salmon steaks are most commonly done on the grill, but to maximize flavor and get the best texture, try this easy sous vide recipe.

INGREDIENTS:

4 thick cut salmon
steaks 2 tablespoons
olive oil 1/2 cup
mayonnaise
1 tablespoon dried
tarragon 3 tablespoons
lemon juice
3 tablespoons Dijon
mustard Salt
Black pepper, finely ground
3 tablespoons granulated sugar

INSTRUCTIONS:

1. Set your Anova to 130F/54.4C.
2. We're going to brine these steaks because it will help reduce the presence of albumin, that unpleasant white stuff that seeps out of salmon.
3. To do this, mix equal parts sugar and salt and coat the salmon steaks completely.
4. Place the steaks in the refrigerator for 10 to 20 minutes and then rinse off the salt and sugar. This should also help the meat stay nice and firm while it cooks.
5. Place the steaks in separate vacuum-sealed bags and submerge in the water bath.
6. Cook for one hour.
7. While the salmon cooks, mix the mayo, tarragon, lemon juice, and mustard in a bowl. Feel free to add a grind or two of pepper if you like.
8. When the salmon is finished cooking, you can either serve it with the

aioli as is or heat a pan with 2 tablespoons of olive oil over high heat or give the steaks a quick sear—not more than 2 minutes per side.

9. Spoon a dollop of the aioli on top and serve.

Sous Vide Haddock with Chermoula Sauce

SERVINGS: 4 | PREP TIME: 20 MINUTES | COOK TIME: 30 MINUTES

Chermoula sauce is a rich Moroccan sauce that will liven up any dish.

INGREDIENTS

For Fish:
2 pounds fresh skinless haddock 2 tablespoons olive oil
2 green bell peppers, cut in slices 2 roma tomatoes, cut into rounds 2 tablespoons lemon juice

For Chermoula Sauce:
1/2 cup coarsely chopped fresh cilantro
1/2 cup coarsely chopped fresh flat-leaf parsley 5 garlic cloves, coarsely chopped
1/3 cup fresh lemon juice 2 teaspoons sweet paprika 2 teaspoons salt
1-1/2 teaspoons ground cumin 1/4 teaspoon cayenne
1/2 cup olive oil

INSTRUCTIONS:

1. Set your Anova to 132F/55.6 C.
2. Arrange the haddock in a vacuum-sealed bag so that it is one

layer. Then add the sliced peppers and tomatoes to the bag.
Drizzle in the olive oil and seal.
3. Submerge the bag in the water bath and cook for 30 minutes.
4. While the fish cooks, combine the sauce ingredients in the bowl of a
   food processor and puree. Add in the olive oil as you puree the rest
   of

   the ingredients.
5. When the fish is finished cooking, remove it from the water bath
   and serve the fish on a bed of the peppers and tomatoes and topped
   with the sauce.

Nutritional Info: Calories: 1031, Sodium: 1181mg, Dietary Fiber: 3.0g, Total
Fat: 33.1g, Total Carbs: 9.4g, Protein: 2.1g.

Sous Vide Salmon and Broccoli Tagliatelle

SERVINGS: 4 | PREP TIME: 20 MINUTES | COOK TIME: 30 MINUTES

This delicious and healthy dish is easy to make, and thanks to your
Vacuum sealer, it's also easy to store leftovers.

INGREDIENTS:

1 package dry tagliatelle
2/3 pounds broccoli, cut into small pieces
1 pound skinless, boneless salmon filets, cut into
chunks 1/2 cup dry white wine
2 tablespoons butter
1 cup onion, thinly
sliced 2/3 heavy cream
1 tablespoon fresh dill, for
garnish Salt & pepper to taste

INSTRUCTIONS:

1. Set your Anova for 130F/54.4C.
2. Boil a large pot of salted water.
3. Chop the salmon into two inch chunks, place in a vacuum-sealed
   bag with the wine, onion, butter and broccoli. Then seal and

submerge in the water bath, cooking for 30 minutes.

4. While the salmon and broccoli cook, put the tagliatelle in the boiling water and cook based on package directions and drain, reserving 1/2 cup of the cooking liquid.

5. When salmon and pasta are both finished cooking, heat a large saucepan over medium heat and combine the pasta with the salmon mixture.

6. Add the reserved pasta water and the heavy cream. Simmer for several minutes until the sauce has thickened slightly and coated the pasta and fish.

7. This recipe may be too much food for two people so if there are any leftovers, just place everything in a vacuum-sealed bag.

8. When ready to eat again, simply set your Anova to 130F/54.4C and reheat for 30 minutes.

Nutritional Info: Calories: 428, Sodium: 175mg, Dietary Fiber: 2.8g, Total Fat: 21.2g, Total Carbs: 27.5g, Protein: 28.8g.

Sous Vide Fish Tacos with Pineapple Salsa

SERVINGS: 6 | PREP TIME: 15 MINUTES | COOK TIME: 30 MINUTES

This refreshing fish taco recipe is full of bright flavors and just the right amount of spice. Thanks to your Anova, it is guaranteed to come out tender and juicy.

INGREDIENTS:

1-1/2 pounds cod
1/2 teaspoon adobo
seasoning 1/2 teaspoon chili
powder
1/2 fresh
pineapple 1
teaspoon sugar
1 tablespoon red onion,
chopped 2 tablespoons
cilantro, chopped Juice of 1

lime
Salt
1 tablespoon vegetable oil
12 soft flour or corn
tortillas 1 avocado, sliced
2 tablespoons sour cream

INSTRUCTIONS:

1. Set your Anova to 135F/57.2C.
2. Season the fish with the adobo seasoning and chili powder.
3. Place the fish in vacuum-sealed bags and submerge in the water bath for 30 minutes.
4. While the fish is cooking, dice the pineapple and mix with the sugar, onion, lime juice, cilantro and a pinch of chili powder.
5. When the fish is almost finished cooking, heat a pan over medium heat.
6. Remove the fish from the water and cook in the pan until just browned.
7. Remove from heat and chop the fish.
8. Heat the tortillas until warm, and top with fish.
9. Serve the salsa either on the side or on top of the fish for a festive taco dinner.

Nutritional Info: Calories: 335, Sodium: 145mg, Dietary Fiber: 5.9g, Total Fat: 12.1g, Total Carbs: 28.5g, Protein: 29.6g.

Sous Vide Prawns with Spicy Peanut Noodles

SERVINGS: 4 | PREP TIME: 20 MINUTES | COOK TIME: 30 MINUTES

Spice up traditional pasta and shrimp with this easy Asian inspired dish. Best of all, the noodles can be made ahead of time and chilled for a refreshing summer dinner.

INGREDIENTS:

1 pound large prawns or shrimp, peeled and
deveined 2 cloves garlic, crushed
1 teaspoon cayenne pepper
1 tablespoon cilantro,

chopped 2 tablespoon lemon
juice
Salt
Ground black
pepper 1 package
spaghetti
2 tablespoons creamy peanut
butter 2 tablespoons toasted
sesame oil
2 tablespoons vegetable oil

INSTRUCTIONS:

1. Set your Anova to 149F/65C.
2. Place prawns in a vacuum-sealed bag with the garlic, cilantro, lemon juice, salt, and pepper.
3. Submerge in the water bath and cook for 15 minutes.
4. While the prawns cook, heat a pot of salted water to boiling and add the spaghetti. Cook according to package directions, run under cold water until the noodles are cool, and drain.
5. In a large bowl mix together the noodles with the peanut butter, sesame oil, and cayenne pepper. If you prefer more heat, add another pinch of cayenne pepper. Chill in the refrigerator for 20 minutes.
6. When the prawns are finished in the water bath, heat a skillet with the vegetable oil to high heat, and quickly sear the shrimp for no more than 30 seconds.
7. Remove from heat and serve the prawns on a bed of the cold noodles.

Nutritional Info: Calories: 488, Sodium: 332mg, Dietary Fiber: 0.7g, Total Fat: 21.1g, Total Carbs: 38.4g, Protein: 35.1g.

Sous Vide Sea Scallops

SERVINGS: 4 | PREP TIME: 10 MINUTES | COOK TIME: 30 MINUTES

Diver scallops are delicious, but they can be a challenge. This recipe will teach you to make foolproof scallops using your Anova.

INGREDIENTS:

12 huge ocean

scallops 1
tablespoon olive oil
1 tablespoons
spread Salt and
pepper

INSTRUCTIONS:

1. Set your Anova to 123F/51C.
2. Place the scallops in a solitary layer inside a vacuum-fixed bag.
3. Submerge the pack in the water shower and cook for 30 minutes. This will not totally cook the scallops which is great since we will burn them in a pan.
4. When the scallops are done in the water shower, heat a huge hardened steel dish on high hotness and add the butter.
5. Remove the scallops from the pack and dry totally with paper towels. This is vital to get a decent sear.
6. When the skillet is practically smoking, add the scallops and singe for 20 seconds on each side.
7. Remove from the container and serve immediately.

Nutritional Info: Calories: 135, Sodium: 165mg, Dietary Fiber: 0g, Total Fat: 7.1g, Total Carbs: 2.1g, Protein: 15.1g.

Sous Vide Miso Cod

SERVINGS: 2 | PREP TIME: 20 MINUTES | COOK TIME: 30 MINUTES

Miso glue is a superb method for adding complex flavor to many dishes. This formula will tell you the best way to make your cod truly come alive.

INGREDIENTS:

1 pound pacific or dark
cod 1/3 cup white miso
paste
3 tablespoons mirin (Japanese cooking
wine) 2 tablespoons rice vinegar
2 tablespoons earthy
colored sugar 1 bundle
bok choy

2 tablespoons olive
oil Salt and pepper

INSTRUCTIONS:

1. Set your Anova to 132F/55.6C.
2. In a little bowl, join the miso glue, mirin, rice vinegar, and earthy colored sugar. Combine as one and hold 3 tablespoons for later.
3. Season the fish with salt and pepper and seal in a vacuum-fixed sack. Lower the pack in the water shower and cook for 30 minutes. At the point when the fish is done cooking, eliminate from the water bath.
4. In a medium skillet, heat the olive oil over high heat.
5. When the oil is hot, throw in the bok choy alongside the held miso blend and cook just until the bok choy starts to wilt.
6. Divide the bok choy onto plates and top with the cod.

Nutritional Info: Calories: 522, Sodium: 2012mg, Dietary Fiber: 3.3g, Total Fat: 18.9g, Total Carbs: 23.4g, Protein: 58.3g.

Sous Vide Ahi Tuna Steaks

SERVINGS: 2 | PREP TIME: 10 MINUTES | COOK TIME: 30 MINUTES

By delicately cooking Ahi fish in your Anova you can accomplish an awesome harmony between flavor and surface. The ponzu sauce includes an invigorating citrus curve customary soy sauce that perks up numerous dishes.

INGREDIENTS:

1/3 cup honey
1/4 cup ponzu
sauce 1 pound ahi
tuna
2 cups short grain rice, for serving
1 tablespoon toasted sesame seeds, for serving

INSTRUCTIONS:

1. Set your Anova to 120F/48.9C.
2. In a little bowl, join the honey and ponzu sauce.
3. Place the ahi steaks in a vacuum-fixed sack and add the honey

and ponzu mixture.

4. Seal the pack and lower in the water shower for 30 minutes.
5. While the fish cooks, set up the rice and add the sesame seeds.
6. Remove the fish from the water shower, cut, and serve promptly with the rice.

Nutritional Info: Calories: 1305, Sodium: 805mg, Dietary Fiber: 3.0g, Total Fat: 21.8g, Total Carbs: 197.5g, Protein: 74.3g.

CHAPTER 12
LAMB

Sous Vide Spiced Lamb Kebabs

SERVINGS: 4 | PREP TIME: 15 MINUTES | COOK TIME: 1-1/2 HOURS

With your sous vide, you needn't bother with a barbecue to make delicious and succulent kebabs. Essentially follow these means and open a completely better approach to make this center eastern favorite.

INGREDIENTS:

2 garlic cloves,

minced Sea salt
Freshly ground dark
pepper 1 teaspoon dried
oregano
1 tablespoon olive oil
4 sheep steaks cut into 2 inch chunks
2 red peppers, deseeded and cut into
pieces 1 huge onion, cut into chunks
2 lemons, cut into
wedges 6 steel or
bamboo skewers

INSTRUCTIONS:

1. Set your Anova to 140F/60C.
2. In an enormous bowl join the garlic, salt, pepper, oregano, olive oil, and sheep lumps. Mix completely to coat.
3. Spoon the sheep into a vacuum-fixed bag.
4. Submerge in the water shower and cook for 1-1/2 hours.
5. When the sheep is nearly gotten done with cooking, heat your broiler to 500F.
6. Remove the sack from the water and wipe sheep off with a paper towel.
7. Skewer the sheep, rotating sheep, pepper, and onion chunks.
8. Arrange the sticks on a baking sheet and cook in the stove for 5 minutes. Eliminate from the stove, turn the sticks and cook and extra 5 minutes. The high hotness of the broiler should give the kebabs a pleasant sear.
9. Serve with the lemon wedges.

Nutritional Info: Calories: 667, Sodium: 486mg, Dietary Fiber: 1.4g, Total Fat: 27.7g, Total Carbs: 6.6g, Protein: 92.8g.

Sous Vide Tandoori Lamb Chops

SERVINGS: 8 | PREP TIME: 2-1/2 HOURS | COOK TIME: 2-3 HOURS

For a great contort on conventional sheep hacks, attempt this Indian motivated rub for delightful outcomes. Garam Masala is the base for many popular Indian dishes like Chicken Tikka Masala and will give your meat dishes an amazing burst of deep flavor.

INGREDIENTS:

8 sheep rib hacks (2-1/2
pounds) 3/4 cups Greek yogurt
1/4 cup weighty cream
3 tablespoons new lemon juice
1 (3-inch piece) new ginger, stripped and
minced 4 huge garlic cloves, minced
1 tablespoon malt vinegar
1 tablespoon garam
masala 1 tablespoon
ground cumin 1
tablespoon paprika
1/2 teaspoon cayenne
pepper Salt

INSTRUCTIONS:

1. Set your Anova to 135F/57.2C.
2. In a huge bowl, whisk the yogurt with the weighty cream, lemon juice, ginger, garlic, malt vinegar, garam masala, cumin, paprika, cayenne, and 1 teaspoon of salt.
3. Place sheep cleaves in a huge vacuum-fixed pack or spot a few slashes in more modest bags.
4. Pour the yogurt marinade over the sheep and seal utilizing your vacuum-sealed.
5. Place the sack in the fridge to marinate for 2 hours.
6. When your water shower is prepared, lower the sack and cook for somewhere around 2 hours and not more than 3 hours.
7. When the sheep is practically gotten done, heat your broiler to 450F.
8. Remove the sheep from the pack and move to a baking sheet.
9. Cook in the stove for 6 minutes and turn the slashes over. Cook 6 extra minutes and serve.

Nutritional Info: Calories: 308, Sodium: 122mg, Dietary Fiber: 0.6g, Total Fat: 12.7g, Total Carbs: 3.1g, Protein: 42.9g.

Sous Vide Shawarma Leg of Lamb

SERVINGS: 6 | PREP TIME: 10 MINUTES | COOK TIME: 14 HOURS

This Middle Eastern enhanced leg of lamb cooks low and slow flawlessly. The mix of colorful flavors is the ideal supplement to this conventional Middle Eastern favorite.

INGREDIENTS:

1 (5-pound) bone-in leg of
sheep, Salt, newly ground
pepper
2 tablespoons   cumin
seeds   2   teaspoons
caraway   seeds   2
teaspoons coriander seeds
2 Thai chilies, finely cleaved 4
garlic cloves, finely grated
1/2 cup olive oil
1 tablespoon paprika
1/2 teaspoon ground cinnamon

INSTRUCTIONS:

1. Set your Anova to 143F/62C.
2. In an enormous bowl join, salt, pepper, cumin, caraway,
   coriander, chilies, garlic, olive oil, paprika, and cinnamon.
3. Rub the combination all around the sheep and spot in a vacuum-fixed
   bag.
4. Seal the pack with your Foodsaver or any vacuum sealer accessible
   and place in the cooler for 2 hours.
5. Submerge the sheep in the water shower and cook for 12 hours.
   For a significantly more delicate surface cook 6 extra hours.

Nutritional Info: Calories: 864, Sodium: 319mg, Dietary Fiber: 1.1g, Total
Fat: 45.2g, Total Carbs: 2.8g, Protein: 107g.

Sous Vide Herbed Lamb Chops

SERVINGS: 6 | PREP TIME: 1 HOUR | COOK TIME: 2-4 HOURS

This is a basic and tasty approach to getting ready sheep cleaves with simply
a smidgen of heat.

INGREDIENTS:

4 huge garlic cloves, pressed
1 tablespoon new thyme leaves, gently crushed

1 tablespoon new rosemary leaves, daintily
squashed 1 teaspoon cayenne pepper
2 teaspoons coarse salt
2 tablespoons extra-virgin olive oil,
partitioned 6 (1-1/4-inch thick) sheep
midsection chops

INSTRUCTIONS:

1. Set your Anova to 135F/57.2C.
2. In a vacuum-fixed pack consolidate the spices, cayenne
   pepper, salt, pepper, oil, and sheep chops.
3. Seal the sack and permit to marinate in the cooler for 1 hour.
4. Submerge in the water shower and cook for something like 2 hours
   and not over 4 hours. At the point when cleaves are practically
   gotten done, heat a skillet over high heat.
5. Remove hacks from the sack and singe for 3 minutes for every
   side before serving.
6. These slashes pair well with a broiled garlic crushed potato.

Nutritional Info: Calories: 205, Sodium: 841mg, Dietary Fiber: 0.5g, Total
Fat: 11.1g, Total Carbs: 1.5g, Protein: 24.1g.

Sous Vide Lamb Casserole

SERVINGS: 6 | PREP TIME: 20 MINUTES | COOK TIME: 2-4 HOURS

This is an antiquated treat that is incredible for heating up on cool days.
What's more since you're not cooking in the broiler, you don't need to
continually watch out for your diner.

INGREDIENTS:

2 tablespoons
flour Salt and
pepper
1-1/2 pounds sheep neck filet,
diced 2 tablespoons vegetable oil
1 medium onion
1 carrot, stripped and diced
1 teaspoon   ground
cinnamon   28   ounces

cleaved tomatoes 2
teaspoons honey
2 cups chicken or sheep
stock 1/2 pound little red
potatoes 1 bundle frozen
peas

INSTRUCTIONS:

1. Set your Anova to 180F/82.2C.
2. Combine the salt, pepper, and flour and throw the sheep parts of coat. Then, at that point, in a medium skillet heat the oil.
3. Brown the sheep on all sides and eliminate from heat.
4. Add the onion and carrots to the dish and cook for 5 minutes, until delicately seared. Throw in the cinnamon.
5. Transfer the sheep, vegetables, and all leftover fixings to a vacuum-fixed bag.
6. Submerge the sack in the water shower and cook for something like 2 and not more than 4 hours.
7. Remove the pack from the water and empty substance into a meal dish. The fluid clinched ought to have thickened into a pleasant smooth gravy.

Nutritional Info: Calories: 434, Sodium: 163mg, Dietary Fiber: 5.5g, Total Fat: 14.7g, Total Carbs: 24.1g, Protein: 50g.

Sous Vide Lamb Loin with Cherry-Balsamic Sauce

SERVINGS: 2 | PREP TIME: 10 MINUTES | COOK TIME: 2-4 HOURS

This delicate, succulent sheep midsection works out in a good way for a rich cherry sauce that you can make in your sous vide as well.

INGREDIENTS:

1 (1-pound) boneless sheep flank
broil Salt and newly ground dark
pepper
1 tablespoon cleaved in addition to 2 entire branches
new rosemary 2 tablespoons unsalted butter

1 medium red onion, daintily sliced
1/2 pound new cherries, hollowed and
slashed 1/4 cup balsamic vinegar

INSTRUCTIONS:

1. Set your Anova to 134F/57C.
2. Season the sheep with salt, pepper and one twig of rosemary, seal in a vacuum-fixed pack and lower in the water shower for somewhere around 2 hours and not more than 4.
3. While the sheep cooks, consolidate the margarine, onion, cherries, and vinegar in another vacuum-fixed bag.
4. An hour prior to the sheep has gotten done, add the sauce sack to the water shower and cook until the sheep is done.
5. Remove the two sacks from the water bath.
6. Slice the sheep into 3/4-inch-thick pieces and top with sauce.

Nutritional Info: Calories: 691, Sodium: 280mg, Dietary Fiber: 3.0g, Total Fat: 28.7g, Total Carbs: 38.9g, Protein: 65.0g.

Simple Sous Vide Rack of Lamb

SERVINGS: 2 | PREP TIME: 1 HOUR | COOK TIME: 2-4 HOURS

Cooking an entire rack of sheep can be interesting, however your sous vide eliminates all the mystery. What's more in light of the fact that the Foodsaver does such a fantastic occupation of making a vacuum seal, your sheep rack will be cooked to even perfection.

INGREDIENTS:

2 racks of sheep,
managed 1 clove
garlic, minced
2 teaspoons salt
1/3 cup new rosemary leaves
1/2 teaspoon newly ground dark pepper
2 teaspoons extra-virgin olive oil

INSTRUCTIONS:

1. Set your Anova to 134F/56.5C.
2. Combine the garlic, salt, rosemary leaves, and pepper, and rub all

around the racks.

3. Place the racks into isolated vacuum-fixed sacks. Marinate the packs in the cooler for 1 hour prior to lowering in the water bath.
4. Cook the racks in the water shower for between 2 to 4 hours.
5. When the sheep is practically done, heat your broiler to 450F.
6. Remove the racks from the vacuum-fixed sacks and spot on a baking sheet or simmering pan.
7. Roast in the stove for around 10 minutes. Eliminate from the stove and serve immediately.

Nutritional Info: Calories: 224, Sodium: 2392mg, Dietary Fiber: 4.3g, Total Fat: 12g, Total Carbs: 7g, Protein: 23.1g.

Sous Vide Slow Cooked Lamb Shanks

SERVINGS: 4 | PREP TIME: 10 MINUTES | COOK TIME: 48 HOURS

One of the greatest benefits of sous vide cooking is that you can cook without continually keeping an eye on your food. These legs of lamb cook at an even temperature to deliver ideal tumble off the bone meat.

INGREDIENTS:

2 bone-in legs of
lamb Salt and dark
pepper 6 branches
new thyme
2 cloves garlic, crushed

INSTRUCTIONS:

1. Set your Anova for 143F/62C.
2. Rub the legs of lamb done with the salt and pepper and spot into isolated vacuum-fixed bags.
3. Add three twigs of thyme and one clove of squashed garlic to each bag.
4. Seal the packs and lower in the water shower for 48 hours.
5. When the sheep is almost completed in the water shower, heat your broiler to 500F.
6. Remove the sheep from the sacks and spot on a baking sheet or simmering pan.

7. Cook in the stove for 10 minutes to accomplish a decent sear.
8. At this point the sheep ought to be firm outwardly and tumble off-the-bone delicate on the inside.

Nutritional Info: Calories: 319, Sodium: 127mg, Dietary Fiber: 1.7g, Total Fat: 12.3g, Total Carbs: 3.4g, Protein: 46.4g.

Sous Vide Slow Cooked Lamb Shoulder

SERVINGS: 4 PREP TIME: 10 MINUTES | COOK TIME: 8 HOURS

This cut of sheep can be interesting since, in such a case that it isn't cooked long sufficient it can turn out intense however the even hotness from your sous vide will guarantee that it is tumble off the bone tender.

INGREDIENTS:

1 entire sheep shoulder, deboned Salt and pepper
3 tablespoons olive oil
1 clove of garlic, crushed
Large twig for every thyme, rosemary and mint

INSTRUCTIONS:

1. Set your Anova to 182F/83.3 C.
2. Rub the sheep with salt and pepper, and spot inside a vacuum-fixed pack. Add the garlic, oil, and herbs.
3. Seal the pack and lower in the water shower for 8 hours.
4. When the sheep is nearly completed the process of cooking, heat your grill to high.
5. Remove the sheep from the water shower and spot on a baking sheet, fat side up.
6. Broil for 8 to 10 minutes or until the fat side is crispy.

Nutritional Info: Calories: 329, Sodium: 96mg, Dietary Fiber: 0.7g, Total Fat: 19.9g, Total Carbs: 1.3g, Protein: 35.3g.

Sous Vide Rosemary Lamb Chops

Lamb hacks are an exquisite treat yet cooking them sous vide will secure the entirety of their rich flavor. This formula tells you the best way to utilize spices to raise sheep hacks while as yet holding their complex character.

INGREDIENTS:

1-1/2 teaspoons cleaved new rosemary
1/2 teaspoon salt
1/4 teaspoon newly ground dark pepper
1 garlic clove, minced
8 (3-ounce) sheep rib slashes,
managed 2 teaspoons olive oil

INSTRUCTIONS:

1. Set your Anova to 140F/60C.
2. Place the sheep slashes in a vacuum-fixed pack with the rosemary, salt, and pepper, and seal.
3. Submerge in the water shower and cook for 2 hours.
4. When the sheep is practically gotten done, heat a skillet over medium hotness, and brown the garlic.
5. Add the sheep and cook until the hacks have browned.
6. Remove from hotness and serve immediately.

Nutritional Info: Calories: 679, Sodium: 841mg, Dietary Fiber: 0g, Total Fat: 29.8g, Total Carbs: 1.2g, Protein: 95.7g.

CHAPTER 13
PORK

Sous Vide Carolina Pulled Pork

SERVINGS: 6-8 | PREP TIME: 20 MINUTES | COOK TIME: 24 HOURS

This customary grill most loved stands apart due to its punchy, tart sauce.

INGREDIENTS:

For the pork:
1 (2-3 pounds) pork
shoulder 1 teaspoon gentle
paprika
2 teaspoons light earthy
colored sugar 1-1/2
teaspoons hot paprika 1/2
teaspoon celery salt
1/2 teaspoon garlic salt
1/2 teaspoon dry

mustard
1/2 teaspoon newly ground dark pepper
1/2 teaspoon onion powder
1/4 teaspoon salt

For the Sauce:
1-1/2 cups yellow
mustard 1/2 cup brown
sugar
3/4 cups juice
vinegar 3/4 cups
beer
1 teaspoon new ground
pepper 1/2 teaspoon cayenne
pepper
1-1/2 teaspoons Worcestershire
sauce 2 tablespoons margarine,
melted
1-1/2 teaspoons fluid smoke

INSTRUCTIONS:

1. Set your Anova to 140F/60C.
2. Combine every one of the flavors for the pork in a little bowl and rub
   the combination all around the pork shoulder.
3. Place the pork shoulder in a vacuum-fixed bag.
4. Submerge the sack in the water and cook for 24 hours.
5. To make the sauce, consolidate all sauce fixings in a medium
   pot and hotness over low hotness until just bubbling.
6. Remove the pork from the water shower and spot in an enormous bowl.
7. Pour in the sauce, and with two forks, shred the pork and blend in
   with the sauce.
8. Serve on delicate buns and top with your most loved coleslaw.

Nutritional Info: Calories: 603, Sodium: 757mg, Dietary Fiber: 2.0g, Total
Fat: 41.3g, Total Carbs: 13.6g, Protein: 41.9g.

Sous Vide Barbecue Pork Ribs

SERVINGS: 4 | PREP TIME: 20 MINUTES | COOK TIME: 12 HOURS

Barbecue ribs are a lasting top pick, and this formula will show you the best
way to make ideal ribs without a smoker. Obviously, an incredible rub is the

way to extraordinary ribs.

INGREDIENTS:

2 racks of St. Louis or child back
ribs 1 teaspoon fluid hickory smoke
1/3 cup paprika
1/3 cup dull earthy
colored sugar 1/4 cup
salt
2 tablespoons entire yellow mustard
seed 1 teaspoon newly ground dark
pepper
2 teaspoons granulated garlic
powder 1 tablespoon dried oregano

INSTRUCTIONS:

1. Set your Anova to 165F/74C.
2. Combine the paprika, sugar, salt, mustard seed, pepper, garlic
   powder, and oregano.
3. Remove the silver skin on the rear of the ribs and cut into three or
   four rib sections.
4. Coat the ribs in the flavor blend and spot in a vacuum-fixed bags.
5. Place in the water shower and cook for 12 hours.
6. Remove from the water shower and wipe off with paper towels.
7. Heat your broiler to 300F and cover the racks with your cherished
   grill sauce.
8. Cook ribs in the stove for around 30-40 minutes. A pleasant covering
   of sauce will form.
9. Note: Feel allowed to add more sauce while the ribs are in the
   broiler for considerably more flavor.

Nutritional Info: Calories: 326, Sodium: 77mg, Dietary Fiber: 4.7g, Total
Fat:

14.9g, Total Carbs: 20.6g, Protein: 29.0g.

Sous Vide Adobo Pork Ribs

These delicate ribs are improved with conventional adobo flavors for a punch of flavor that is both tart and spicy.

INGREDIENTS:

1 cup apple juice
vinegar 1 tablespoon
soy sauce
3 inlet leaves
1 enormous jalapeño bean stew, chopped
1 side child back pork ribs, cut into individual
ribs 2 teaspoons ocean salt
6 garlic cloves, peeled
2 teaspoons dark peppercorns

INSTRUCTIONS:

1. Set your Anova to 165F/74C.
2. In a bowl, join the vinegar, soy sauce, straight leaves, and chilies.
3. Season the ribs with salt and spot inside a vacuum-fixed sack with the garlic, pepper, and vinegar blend. Seal the sack and lower in the water shower for 12 hours.
4. When the ribs are almost completed in the water shower, preheat your broiler to 400F.
5. Remove the ribs from the pack and pour 1/4 cup of the fluid over the ribs. Place in the broiler for 10-15 minutes, or until browned.
6. Serve with steamed rice and the leftover cooking liquid.

Nutritional Info: Calories: 520, Sodium: 1381mg, Dietary Fiber: 1.0g, Total Fat: 12.3g, Total Carbs: 1.0g, Protein: 90.0g.

Sous Vide Spicy Korean Pork Ribs

These Korean style ribs sneak up suddenly because of a hot pepper glue known as gochujang. Your Foodsaver will secure in the flavor by making an ideal vacuum seal.

INGREDIENTS:

3 pounds child back pork ribs, isolated into individual ribs
1/2 cup gochujang
2 tablespoons dim earthy
colored sugar 2 tablespoons
soy sauce
2 tablespoons rice vinegar
2 teaspoons toasted sesame
oil Salt to taste

INSTRUCTIONS:

1. Set your Anova to 165F/74C.
2. In a bowl, join the gochujang, earthy colored sugar, soy sauce, vinegar, and sesame oil.
3. Season the ribs with salt and spot in a vacuum-fixed pack. Add the marinade to the sack and seal.
4. Submerge the pack in the water shower and cook for 12 hours.
5. When the ribs are almost gotten done, heat your stove to 450F.
6. Remove the ribs from the sack and save the marinade. Place the ribs on a baking sheet and brush with the saved marinade.
7. Cook in the stove for 15 minutes and treat again with marinade. Cook 10 extra minutes.

Nutritional Info: Calories: 536, Sodium: 1407mg, Dietary Fiber: 0g, Total Fat: 14.3g, Total Carbs: 5.5g, Protein: 89.7g.

Sous Vide Rosemary Lamb Chops

SERVINGS: 2 | PREP TIME: 10 MINUTES | COOK TIME: 2 HOURS

Sheep slashes are an exquisite treat however cooking them sous vide will secure the entirety of their rich flavor. This formula tells you the best way to utilize spices to hoist sheep hacks while as yet holding their complex character.

INGREDIENTS:

8 (3-ounce) sheep rib slashes, trimmed
1-1/2 teaspoons cleaved new rosemary
1/2 teaspoon salt
1/4 teaspoon newly ground dark pepper
1 garlic clove, minced

2 teaspoons olive oil

INSTRUCTIONS:

1. Set your Anova to 140F/60C.
2. Place the sheep hacks in a vacuum-fixed pack with the rosemary, salt, and pepper, and seal.
3. Submerge in the water shower and cook for 2 hours.
4. When the sheep is practically gotten done, heat a skillet over medium hotness, and brown the garlic.
5. Add the sheep and cook until the cleaves have browned.
6. Remove from hotness and serve immediately.

Nutritional Info: Calories: 679, Sodium: 841mg, Dietary Fiber: 0g, Total Fat: 29.8g, Total Carbs: 1.2g, Protein: 95.7g.

Sous Vide Herbed Pork Chops

SERVINGS: 4 | PREP TIME: 10 MINUTES | COOK TIME: 1 HOUR

These hacks are brimming with flavor, and gratitude to your Anova, they're ensured to come out entirely every time.

INGREDIENTS:

4 bone-in pork chops
4 branches new
rosemary 2 cloves
garlic, squashed 2
tablespoons olive oil
2 tablespoons spread
Salt and pepper

INSTRUCTIONS:

1. Heat your Anova to 140F/60C for medium uncommon slashes. For medium well, set your Anova to 150F/66C.
2. Place the hacks, spices, salt, pepper, and spread in a vacuum-fixed bag.
3. Submerge in the water shower for something like 1 hour and not more than 4.
4. When the slashes are almost gotten done, heat a skillet (ideally cast iron) on high hotness with the olive oil.
5. Remove cleaves from the sack and burn rapidly on both side until a

pleasant hull is achieved.

6. Remove from the container and serve immediately.

Nutritional Info: Calories: 370, Sodium: 97mg, Dietary Fiber: 0g, Total Fat: 32.5g, Total Carbs: 0.6g, Protein: 18.2g.

Sous Vide Cochinita Pibil

SERVINGS: 6 | PREP TIME: 15 MINUTES | COOK TIME: 12-24 HOURS

Cochinita Pibil is a Mayan style pit pork that is cooked low and slow to delicate perfection.

INGREDIENTS:

1 boneless pork shoulder
3/4 cups disintegrated achiote
glue 3 tablespoons orange
juice
1 tablespoon white wine
vinegar 2 garlic cloves, minced
1/4 teaspoons dried oregano
3 medium yellow onions,
quartered 1/2 cup water

INSTRUCTIONS:

1. Set your Anova to 158F/70C.
2. Combine the achiote glue, squeezed orange, vinegar, garlic, and oregano in a bowl and blend well.
3. Season the pork shoulder with the combination so it is completely coated.
4. Place the pork in a vacuum-fixed pack with the quartered onions, water, and remaining flavoring mixture.
5. Seal the sack and lower in the water shower for 12 to 24 hours.
6. Remove the pork from the water shower, empty whole substance into an enormous bowl.
7. Using forks, shred the pork and onions, and blend in with the cooking fluid. The pork ought to be really delicate that it self-destructs easily.
8. Serve with salsa and corn tortillas.

Nutritional Info: Calories: 405, Sodium: 776mg, Dietary Fiber: 1.2g, Total Fat: 34.6g, Total Carbs: 6.3g, Protein: 97.9g.

Sous Vide Herbed Pork Roast

SERVINGS: 6 | PREP TIME: 10 MINUTES | COOK TIME: 2-4 HOURS

Pork broil is a conventional top pick, yet in any event, cooking can be troublesome. On account of your Anova, you can have impeccably cooked meals each time.

INGREDIENTS:

1 (5 pound) boneless pork flank 1 teaspoon scoured sage
1/2 teaspoon salt
1/4 teaspoon pepper
1 clove garlic, squashed 1/2 cup sugar
1 tablespoon cornstarch 1/4 cup vinegar
1/4 cup water
2 tablespoons soy sauce

INSTRUCTIONS:

1. Set your Anova to 140F/60C.
2. In a bowl, join the wise, salt, pepper, and garlic.
3. Rub the blend generously on the pork and spot in a vacuum-fixed bag.
4. Submerge the sack in the water shower and cook for somewhere around 2 hours and not more than 4.
5. When the pork is almost gotten done, heat your broiler to 450F.
6. In a pot, consolidate the sugar, cornstarch, vinegar, water, and soy sauce.
7. Cook over medium hotness until the sauce has diminished and somewhat thickened.
8. Remove the pork from the water shower and spot on a baking

sheet or simmering pan.

9. Baste with the combination and spot in the stove for 20 minutes.
10. Remove cook from the stove and cut into 1/2-inch-thick pieces.

Nutritional Info: Calories: 989, Sodium: 730mg, Dietary Fiber: 0g, Total Fat: 52.6g, Total Carbs: 18.7g, Protein: 103.6g.

Sous Vide Espresso-Chili Ribs

SERVINGS: 6 | PREP TIME: 10 MINUTES | COOK TIME: 12 HOURS

Espresso isn't only for drinking. As this formula will illustrate, it can make for a profoundly delightful option to a conventional zest rub.

INGREDIENTS:

4 pounds child back pork
ribs 2 tablespoons cayenne
pepper 1 tablespoon paprika
1 tablespoon ground
cumin 1-1/2 teaspoons
salt
3/4 teaspoons ground dark
pepper 1 (12-ounce) bottle dull
lager Your cherished grill sauce
1/2 cup water
2 tablespoons light brown sugar
1 tablespoon moment coffee powder

INSTRUCTIONS:

1. Set your Anova to 165F/74C.
2. In a little bowl, join the cayenne pepper, paprika, cumin, salt, and pepper.
3. Rub the zest blend on the ribs, covering completely.
4. Place the ribs in a vacuum-fixed sack however don't seal it yet.
5. In a little pan, diminish the brew by about half and fill the pack with the ribs and afterward seal.
6. Submerge the pack in the water shower and cook for 12 hours.
7. When the ribs are almost completed the process of cooking, consolidate the grill sauce, water, earthy colored sugar, and coffee powder in a medium pot over low heat.
8. Remove the ribs from the water shower and wipe off with paper towels.

9. Heat your broiler to 400F and brush the grill sauce combination over the ribs.
10. Place the ribs on a baking sheet and cook in the stove for 10 minutes.
11. Brush one more covering of sauce onto the ribs and cook 10 extra minutes.
12. Note: Serve ribs with the leftover grill sauce on the side.

Nutritional Info: Calories: 482, Sodium: 760mg, Dietary Fiber: 1.1g, Total Fat: 11.3g, Total Carbs: 7.2g, Protein: 80g.

Sous Vide Pork Medallions with Fennel

SERVINGS: 6 | PREP TIME: 10 MINUTES | COOK TIME: 2 HOURS

Fennel cooked low and slow in the sous vide can open its perplexing flavors. What's more it tends to be cooked simultaneously as the pork medallions.

INGREDIENTS:

1-1/2 pounds pork flank, cut into emblems Salt and ground pepper
4 tablespoons olive oil, in addition to additional for serving 2 fennel bulbs, managed and daintily cut Juice of 1/2 lemon
1 branch new thyme
1 spring new oregano
2 cloves garlic, stripped and delicately squashed Chopped new parsley, for serving

INSTRUCTIONS:

1. Set your Anova to 140F/60C.
2. Rub the pork with salt and pepper, and 1 tablespoon of oil, and spot in one vacuum-fixed bag.
3. In another vacuum-fixed sack, consolidate 1 tablespoon of oil, fennel, lemon juice, thyme, oregano, and garlic. Lower the two sacks in the water shower and cook for 2 hours.

4. Just prior to eliminating the packs from the water shower, heat an enormous skillet on medium hotness and add the leftover oil.
5. Place the pork emblems and the fennel combination in the container and cook the pork for 2 minutes for each side.
6. Remove from hotness and embellishment with new parsley.

Sous Vide Indian Spiced Pork Meatballs

SERVINGS: 8 | PREP TIME: 15 MINUTES | COOK TIME: 1 HOUR

Cooking meatballs sous vide guarantees rich flavor just as ensured tenderness.

INGREDIENTS:

1 pound ground pork
1 egg, delicately beaten
1/3 cup bread crumbs
1 red bean stew, cultivated and finely hacked
2 teaspoons ground new ginger
1 onion, grated
1 teaspoon garam masala
2 tablespoons cleaved new cilantro
Sea salt and ground pepper
1 tablespoon vegetable oil

INSTRUCTIONS:

1. Set your Anova to 140F/60C.
2. In a huge bowl, consolidate pork, onion, egg, bread morsels, stew, ginger, garam masala, cilantro, salt, and pepper and blend well.
3. Using a spoon, shape the blend into little balls and spot inside a vacuum-fixed bag.
4. Seal the pack and lower in the water shower, cooking for something

like 1 hour and not more than 3.

5. When the meatballs are almost gotten done, heat a huge skillet over high hotness and add the oil.
6. Remove the meatballs from the sack and spot in the skillet, cooking until they are simply browned.
7. Remove and serve immediately.

Nutritional Info: Calories: 130, Sodium: 106mg, Dietary Fiber: 0.6g, Total

Fat: 4.5g, Total Carbs: 5.1g, Protein: 16.4g.

Sous Vide Five Spice Pork Tenderloin

SERVINGS: 6 | PREP TIME: 10 MINUTES | COOK TIME: 2 HOURS

This formula utilizes a customary Chinese zest mix to add profound, rich flavor to a pork tenderloin.

INGREDIENTS:

1-1/2 pounds pork tenderloin
1 tablespoon five-zest
powder 1 teaspoon dry
mustard
1/2 teaspoon ground
ginger 1/2 teaspoon
pepper
1/2 teaspoon salt
2 tablespoons nut oil
1/3 cup hoisin sauce

INSTRUCTIONS:

1. Set your Anova to 140F/60C.
2. In a little bowl, join the five zest powder, mustard, ginger, salt, and pepper.
3. Rub the zest blend on the pork flank and seal in a vacuum-fixed sack. Lower the pack and cook for 2 hours.
4. When the pork is almost gotten done, heat your stove to 450F.

5. Remove the pork from the sack and spot on a baking sheet.
6. Roast in the stove for 10 minutes, or barely enough an ideal opportunity for the outside to brown slightly.
7. Remove from the stove, cut, and present with hoisin sauce.

Nutritional Info: Calories: 241, Sodium: 488mg, Dietary Fiber: 1.1g, Total Fat: 9.1g, Total Carbs: 7.0g, Protein: 30.6g.

Simple Sous Vide Pork Belly

SERVINGS: 4 | PREP TIME: 10 MINUTES | COOK TIME: 7-8 HOURS

Sous vide is the best technique for impeccably cooked pork paunch, and this formula will show you the insider facts of adding considerably more flavor politeness of your Foodsaver and the right seasonings.

INGREDIENTS:

1 pound pork belly
1 clove garlic,
squashed 3/4 cups dry
white wine 1/4 cup
soy sauce
Salt
Black pepper

INSTRUCTIONS:

1. Set your Anova at 176F/80C.
2. Combine all fixings in a vacuum-fixed bag.
3. Submerge pack in water shower and cook for 7 to 8 hours.
4. Remove the sack and save the fluid from the bag.
5. Pour the fluid in a pot and diminish by about half until the fluid has thickened.
6. Glaze the pork midsection with the sauce, cut, and serve.

Nutritional Info: Calories: 550, Sodium: 2732mg, Dietary Fiber: 0g, Total Fat: 30.6g, Total Carbs: 2.1g, Protein: 53.4g.

CHAPTER 14
BEEF

The Ultimate Sous Vide Meatloaf

SERVINGS: 6 | PREP TIME: 30 MINUTES | COOK TIME: 2 HOURS

This isn't only a meatloaf formula, it's conceivably the most tasty meatloaf formula ever, and gratitude to your Anova, it will be cooked to perfection.

INGREDIENTS:

2 tablespoons olive oil
1/2 yellow onion, stripped and diced
1/4 yellow chime pepper, cultivated and diced 1/4 green ringer pepper, cultivated and diced 1/4 red chime pepper, cultivated and diced 1/2 cup tomato, pureed
2 enormous eggs
1/4 cup weighty cream
1 tablespoons Worcestershire

sauce 1 teaspoons ocean salt
1/2 teaspoon ground dark
pepper 1/2 teaspoon paprika
1/4 teaspoon garlic
powder 1/2 pound ground
sirloin 1/2 ground pork
1/4 sweet Italian sausage

INSTRUCTIONS:

1. Set your Anova to 140F/60C.
2. In a Medium pot, heat the olive oil over medium hotness, and add
    the onions, peppers, and tomato.
3. Cook until peppers and onions are soft.
4. In a huge bowl, join the eggs, cream, onions and peppers, and all of
    the seasonings.
5. Finally, add the ground meat and mix until it is well combined.
6. Pour blend into a huge vacuum-fixed bag.
7. Seal the pack so an essential portion shape is kept up with at the base
    and

    lower it in the water shower for somewhere around 2, however not a
    bigger number of than 6 hours.
8. When the meatloaf is almost gotten done, heat your oven to high.
9. Remove the meatloaf from the pack and spot on a baking sheet
    or simmering pan.
10. Broil for 5 minutes and flip.
11. Broil for an additional 5 minutes and eliminate from the broiler.

Nutritional Info: Calories: 299, Sodium: 660mg, Dietary Fiber: 0.8g, Total
Fat: 16.1g, Total Carbs: 4.3g, Protein: 33.4g.

Sous Vide Spice Rubbed Filet Mignon

SERVINGS: 4 | PREP TIME: 10 MINUTES | COOK TIME: 45
MINUTES

Filet is a rich cut yet without some additional flavor it tends to be a piece
dull. Typically filet is joined by a rich sauce, yet a zest rub is far superior for
cajoling out the sensitive kind of the meat.

INGREDIENTS:

4 thick cut filets
2 tablespoons paprika
2 tablespoons ground
cumin 2 tablespoons dry
mustard
1 tablespoon dark
pepper 2 tablespoons
salt
2 tablespoons butter

INSTRUCTIONS:

1. Set your Anova to 135F/57.2C for medium or 125F/51.6C for medium rare.
2. In a bowl, consolidate the paprika, cumin, mustard, salt, and pepper.
3. Rub the filets with the zest mix and spot in individual vacuum-fixed bags.
4. Submerge the sacks in the water shower and cook for somewhere around 45 minutes and not more than 2 hours.
5. When the filets are done in the water shower, heat an enormous cast iron dish over high heat.
6. Sear the filets for 2 minutes for each side and afterward add the spread and cook for 2 extra minutes. Eliminate from the dish and serve immediately.

Nutritional Info: Calories: 260, Sodium: 2912mg, Dietary Fiber: 0g, Total Fat: 13.8g, Total Carbs: 6.2g, Protein: 28.5g.

Sous Vide Keema

SERVINGS: 6 | PREP TIME: 20 MINUTES | COOK TIME: 45 MINUTES

This Pakistani ground hamburger goulash highlights unpretentious flavors that make a daring eating experience that can be ready in under an hour utilizing your Anova.

INGREDIENTS:

1-1/2 pounds lean ground
sirloin 1 cup hacked onions

2 cups canned squashed
tomatoes 1 cup frozen peas
1 cup diced potatoes
1/2 teaspoon every cinnamon, turmeric,
ginger 1 tablespoon curry powder
Salt
Ground dark pepper

INSTRUCTIONS:

1. Set your Anova to 140F/65C.
2. In a huge skillet, brown the meat and add the onions, cooking until
    the meat is browned.
3. Place the hamburger and onions in a vacuum-fixed sack and
    add the tomatoes, peas, potatoes, spices.
4. Seal the pack and lower in the water shower for 45 minutes.
5. Remove the sack from the water, season with salt and pepper and
    serve over rice.

Nutritional Info: Calories: 149, Sodium: 206mg, Dietary Fiber: 5.7g, Total
Fat: 4.4g, Total Carbs: 17.3g, Protein: 10.7g.

Sous Vide Chili Con Carne

SERVINGS: 8 | PREP TIME: 20 MINUTES | COOK TIME: 12 HOURS

This is potentially the simplest stew formula ever, and in light of the fact
that your Anova keeps everything at an even temperature, you don't
need to mind it.

INGREDIENTS:

1 tablespoon oil
1 enormous onion
1 red pepper, sliced
2 garlic cloves, peeled
1   teaspoon   hot   cayenne
pepper 1 tablespoon gentle
bean stew powder 1 teaspoon
paprika
1 teaspoon   ground
cumin 1 pound lean

ground hamburger 1
cup hamburger stock or
broth
3/4 pounds cleaved
tomatoes 1 teaspoon sugar
2 tablespoons tomato
purée 3/4 pounds red
kidney beans

INSTRUCTIONS:

1. Set your Anova to 170F/76C.
2. In a huge skillet heat the oil and add the garlic, onion and red
   pepper, cooking until they become straightforward. Add the
   cayenne pepper, stew powder, paprika, cumin, and meat broth.
3. Simmer for 5 minutes and fill a huge vacuum-fixed bag.
4. In a similar skillet, brown the hamburger and add the tomatoes.
5. Add the hamburger combination to the vacuum-fixed pack
   alongside the sugar, tomato puree, and beans.
6. Seal the sack and lower in the water shower for 12 hours.
7. Remove the sack from the water and serve bean stew over rice.

Nutritional Info: Calories: 294, Sodium: 154mg, Dietary Fiber: 8.2g, Total
Fat: 6.2g, Total Carbs: 32.1g, Protein: 28.2g.

Sous Vide Mongolian Beef

SERVINGS: 4 | PREP TIME: 20 MINUTES | COOK TIME: 1 HOUR

A top pick at Chinese eateries, this Mongolian meat is made considerably
more delicate and delightful with the even temperature given by your
Anova. Furthermore since your Foodsaver vows to seal totally without fail,
you can cook the meat in the rich sauce.

INGREDIENTS:

2 teaspoons vegetable oil
1/2 teaspoon minced
ginger 1 tablespoon
hacked garlic 1/2 cup soy
sauce
1/2 cup water
3/4 cups dull earthy

colored sugar 1 pound
flank steak
1/4 cup cornstarch
2 green onions, sliced

INSTRUCTIONS:

1. Set your Anova to 140F/65C.
2. Heat a dish over medium hotness and add the garlic, ginger, soy sauce, and water. Let stew briefly and afterward add the earthy colored sugar. Mix until the sauce thickens slightly.
3. Slice the steak into strips and spot in a vacuum-fixed bag.
4. Pour the sauce into the sack with the hamburger and seal.
5. Submerge in the water shower and cook for 1 hour.
6. Remove from water shower and present with cut green onion and steamed rice.

Nutritional Info: Calories: 397, Sodium: 1871mg, Dietary Fiber: 0.6g, Total Fat: 11.7g, Total Carbs: 37.8g, Protein: 33.9g.

Sous Vide Corned Beef

SERVINGS: 6 | PREP TIME: 30 MINUTES | COOK TIME: 48 HOURS

This customary Irish most loved is not difficult to make in your Anova, and the long cooking time will guarantee profound rich flavor.

INGREDIENTS:

1 (5-pound) meat
brisket 1 cup dull beer
1 cup meat stock
2 tablespoons pickling
zest 1 onion, sliced
1 head cabbage (optional)

INSTRUCTIONS:

1. Set your Anova to 135F/57.2C.
2. Rub the brisket with pickling zest and spot in a vacuum-fixed pack with the brew, meat stock, and onion.
3. Seal the pack and lower in the water shower for 48 hours.
4. Remove from the water shower and cut against the grain.

5. Bonus: If you need to go with your corned meat with braised cabbage, eliminate the brisket from the sack and supplant with slashed cabbage.
6. Mix with the cooking fluid and use your Foodsaver to reseal the pack. Lower in the water shower for 30 minutes and serve.

Nutritional Info: Calories: 759, Sodium: 403mg, Dietary Fiber: 3.5g, Total Fat: 23.8g, Total Carbs: 10.0g, Protein: 117.0g.

Sous Vide Beef Stroganoff

SERVINGS: 6 | PREP TIME: 20 MINUTES | COOK TIME: 1 HOUR

This conventional most loved can be made sous vide for much more delicate hamburger, and since this formula utilizes less oil than most plans, it is likewise a better option.

INGREDIENTS:

1-1/2 pounds sirloin steak, cut into strips
2 cups cut white or Cremini mushrooms
2 onions, sliced
1 clove garlic,
slashed 2 tablespoons
margarine 1/2
teaspoon salt
1-1/2 cups low sodium meat
stock 1 teaspoon Worcestershire
sauce 1/4 cup flour
1 cup fat free sharp cream
3 cups cooked egg noodles

INSTRUCTIONS:

1. Set your Anova to 150F/65.5C.
2. In a medium skillet cook the onions and mushrooms until onions become straightforward and eliminate from heat.
3. Place hamburger in a vacuum-fixed pack with the stock, onion combination, Worcestershire sauce, flour, and acrid cream. Seal the sack and lower in the water shower for 1 hour.
4. While the meat cooks, heat a pot of salted water to the point of boiling, and add the noodles.

5. When the hamburger has completed the process of cooking, eliminate from pack and blend in with the noodles. The sauce ought to be creamy.

Nutritional Info: Calories: 445, Sodium: 536mg, Dietary Fiber: 2.1g, Total Fat: 13.1g, Total Carbs: 35.5g, Protein: 42.3g.

Sous Vide Marinated T-Bone Steaks

SERVINGS: 4 | PREP TIME: 10 MINUTES | COOK TIME: 1 HOUR

An extraordinary marinade can be the key to an amazing steak. This formula will take any slice of hamburger to another degree of flavor.

INGREDIENTS:

4 T-bone steaks
2 cups vegetable oil
1 cup soy sauce
1 cup Worcestershire sauce
1/2 cup pineapple juice
2 tablespoons granulated garlic
2 tablespoons newly ground dark pepper
2 tablespoons dry mustard

INSTRUCTIONS:

1. Combine the oil, soy sauce, Worcestershire sauce, pineapple juice, garlic, pepper, and mustard in a bowl, and refrigerate for 6 hours.
2. Place every steak in a vacuum-fixed pack and pour in a portion of the marinade. Seal the packs and spot in the cooler for one hour.
3. Set your Anova to 125F/51.6C for medium uncommon or 135F/57.2C for medium steaks.
4. Submerge the sacks in the water shower and cook for somewhere around 1 hour and not more than 3 hours.
5. When the steaks are almost gotten done, heat a cast iron skillet on the oven over high hotness until smoking.
6. Remove the steaks from the sack and singe for 3 minutes for every

side, until a dim burn appears.

Sous Vide Barbecue Beef Brisket

SERVINGS: 12 | PREP TIME: 1 HOUR AND 10 MINUTES | COOK TIME: 24-48 HOURS

Brisket can be cooked various ways, yet to get delicate grill style brisket you want to allow it to cook for quite a while. This formula will tell you the best way to utilize your Foodsaver and Anova to make legitimate grill brisket in your home.

INGREDIENTS:

1 (5-pound) meat brisket
4 tablespoons ground cumin
2 tablespoons smoked paprika 2 tablespoons dry mustard
3 tablespoons dim earthy colored sugar 2 tablespoons ground rosemary 1 tablespoon cayenne pepper
3 tablespoons salt
1 cup your beloved grill sauce 2 teaspoons fluid smoke

INSTRUCTIONS:

1. Set your Anova to 137F/58.3C.
2. In a bowl, join the cumin, paprika, mustard, sugar, rosemary, pepper, and salt.
3. Rub the flavor mix all around the brisket and spot in the fridge for one hour.
4. Remove the brisket from the cooler and coat, generously, with half of the grill sauce.
5. Place the brisket in a vacuum-fixed sack and lower in the water shower for 24 to 48 hours. Cooking for 24 hours will yield a firmer brisket, while 48 hours will deliver flakier meat.

6. When the brisket is almost completed the process of cooking, heat your broiler to 450F.
7. Remove the brisket from the water shower, cover with the excess grill sauce and cook in the stove for 10 minutes.
8. Slice the brisket daintily contrary to what would be expected and serve.

Nutritional Info: Calories: 414, Sodium: 2107mg, Dietary Fiber: 1.4g, Total Fat: 13.1g, Total Carbs: 12.5g, Protein: 58.4g.

Sous Vide Korean Short Ribs

SERVINGS: 6 | PREP TIME: 20 MINUTES | COOK TIME: 12 HOURS

Slow cooked short ribs become delicate and tasty in light of the fact that the connective tissue makes some long memories to separate. Cooking short ribs sous vide is the least demanding, most idiot proof approach to accomplishing amazing texture.

INGREDIENTS:

3 pounds short ribs
1/3 cup soy sauce
1/3 cup earthy colored sugar 1/3
cup rice wine
1 tablespoon sesame oil
2 teaspoons dark
pepper 1/4 teaspoon
cayenne
1 medium onion, stripped and
quartered 8 garlic cloves, peeled
1 little Asian pear, shredded
1 (1-inch) lump of ginger,
stripped 2 teaspoons sesame
seeds

INSTRUCTIONS:

1. Combine the soy sauce, earthy colored sugar, rice wine, sesame oil, pepper, cayenne pepper, onion, garlic, pear, ginger, and sesame seeds in a huge bowl.
2. Place the ribs in the bowl and refrigerate for 2 hours.

3. Set your Anova to 185F/85C.
4. Remove the ribs from the marinade and spot straightforwardly into a vacuum-fixed bag.
5. Seal the sack and lower in the water shower for 12 hours.
6. Remove the sack from the water shower and serve the short ribs over steamed rice.

Nutritional Info: Calories: 440, Sodium: 1048mg, Dietary Fiber: 1.7g, Total Fat: 10.9g, Total Carbs: 22.7g, Protein: 61.1g.

Sous Vide Spicy Burger

SERVINGS: 4 | PREP TIME: 30 MINUTES | COOK TIME: 50 MINUTES

This new interpretation of the exemplary burger is loaded with flavor and entirely delicate because of your Anova.

INGREDIENTS:

2 pounds ground chuck
1 tablespoon vegetable oil
1 yellow onion, finely chopped
2 tablespoons minced new
ginger 2 cloves garlic, finely
chopped
2 teaspoons cayenne
pepper 1 teaspoon ground
cumin
1 teaspoon garam
masala 2 teaspoons salt
4 cut pepper jack or cheddar 4
Kaiser rolls

INSTRUCTIONS:

1. Set your Anova to 135F/57.2C.
2. Heat the oil in a pot over medium hotness, and cook the onions, ginger, and garlic until soft.
3. In a huge bowl, join the hamburger with the onion combination and cayenne pepper, cumin, garam masala, and salt. Blend well and structure into 4 patties.

4. Place the patties in a vacuum-fixed sack and lower in the water shower for 45 minutes.
5. When the burgers are almost gotten done with cooking, heat a cast iron dish over high hotness. Eliminate the burgers from the pack, place in the dish, and top with a cut of cheddar. Cook for 5 minutes or until the cheddar starts to liquefy. Present with the kaiser rolls.

Nutritional Info: Calories: 467, Sodium: 1699mg, Dietary Fiber: 2.6g, Total

Fat: 23.8g, Total Carbs: 36.1g, Protein: 26.5g.

Sous Vide Hanger Steak

SERVINGS: 2 | PREP TIME: 15 MINUTES | COOK TIME: 1 HOUR

Hanger steak is simply starting to become famous because of its exceptional solid flavor. This formula will tell you the best way to make impeccably cooked holder steak with a powerful jus.

INGREDIENTS:

1 pound holder
steak 2 tablespoons
salt
2 tablespoons dark
pepper 3 tablespoons
butter
1/2 cup low sodium chicken
stock 1/2 cup red wine
1 twig thyme

INSTRUCTIONS:

1. Set your Anova to 135F/57.2C.
2. Rub the holder steak done with salt and pepper and spot in a vacuum-fixed pack with 1 tablespoon of butter.
3. Seal the sack and spot in the water shower for 45 minutes.
4. While the steak is cooking, heat a container on medium hotness and add the chicken stock, wine, and thyme. Lessen by about half.
5. When the steak is done, eliminate it from the pack and pour the fluid

from the sack into the saucepan.

6. Heat a huge cast iron dish over high hotness and when smoking, add the steak, singing on all sides. Eliminate from the pan.
7. Slice the steak contrary to what would be expected and sprinkle with the jus to serve.

Sous Vide Beef Ribs

SERVINGS: 6 | PREP TIME: 15 MINUTES | COOK TIME: 48 HOURS

Beef ribs are best cooked low and slow for delicate tumble off the bone meat. That can make cooking meat ribs at home a test, however on account of your Anova it's simply an issue of time.

INGREDIENTS:

2 racks
hamburger ribs
4 tablespoons
salt
3 tablespoons dark pepper
2 tablespoons dull earthy
colored sugar 2 teaspoons
cayenne pepper

INSTRUCTIONS:

1. Set your Anova to 135F/57.2C.
2. In a little bowl, join the salt, pepper, sugar, and cayenne.
3. Rub the zest blend on the ribs, covering entirely.
4. Place the ribs in a vacuum-fixed pack and lower in the water shower for 48 hours.
5. When the ribs are almost gotten done, heat your broiler to 500F.
6. Remove the ribs from the sack, place on a baking sheet and cook in the stove for 10-15 minutes to accomplish a decent dim outside layer. Present with your cherished grill sauce.

Sous Vide Beef Stew

SERVINGS: 8 | PREP TIME: 30 MINUTES | COOK TIME: 6 HOURS

Beef stew is a generous winter treat that can be put away effectively in the cooler gratitude to your Foodsaver. This formula will tell you the best way to get the most awesome outcomes by utilizing your Anova rather than a sluggish cooker.

INGREDIENTS:

1 cup thick cut bacon, cut into
lumps 2 tablespoons butter
2 pounds sirloin or toss broil, cut into pieces
2 carrots, cut into chunks
1 yellow onion,
diced 2 cups red
wine
2 cups low sodium
hamburger stock 1
tablespoon tomato paste
1 clove garlic,
cleaved 1 branch new
thyme
1 straight leaf

INSTRUCTIONS:

1. Set your Anova to 140F/60C.
2. Heat a huge skillet over medium hotness and cook the bacon until fat is for the most part delivered. Eliminate the bacon from the skillet and add the hamburger, sautéing on all sides.
3. Add the carrots and onions to the container and cook for around 10 minutes or until the vegetables start to soften.
4. Add the wine, stock, garlic, tomato glue, and thyme to the dish and bring to a boil.
5. Remove the skillet from the hotness and fill an enormous vacuum-fixed bag.
6. Submerge the pack in the water shower and cook for 6 hours.
7. Remove the sack from the water shower and serve. Extras can be resealed in a vacuum-fixed sack and frozen for later.

Nutritional Info: Calories: 457, Sodium: 957mg, Dietary Fiber: 1.0g, Total

Fat: 21.9g, Total Carbs: 5.7g, Protein: 46g.

Sous Vide Classic New York Strip Steak

SERVINGS: 2 | PREP TIME: 10 MINUTES | COOK TIME: 45 MINUTES

The business standard New York Strip has been a top choice of steak experts the world over and numerous steak houses have since a long time ago depended on sous vide cooking to ensure each steak that leaves the kitchen is the ideal temperature. Furthermore genuinely, there is no technique better than sous vide to achieve this.

INGREDIENTS:

2 (12-16 ounces) New York Strip
steaks Salt and dark pepper
2 tablespoons butter
1 tablespoon vegetable oil

INSTRUCTIONS:

1. Set your Anova to 125F/51.6C for medium uncommon or 130F/54.4 for medium.
2. Pat the steaks dry with paper towels and season generously with salt and pepper. Place the steaks on a wire rack and leave, revealed, in the cooler for 60 minutes. They ought to seem dry.
3. Place the steaks in individual vacuum-fixed packs and lower in the water shower for 45 minutes. They can be kept in the shower longer, however not longer than 3 hours. After that point the surface will be affected.
4. When the steaks are almost gotten done, heat a cast iron container on high hotness with the oil until it is smoking.
5. Remove the steaks from the pack and singe for 3 to 4 minutes on each side, adding the spread halfway through.
6. Remove the steaks from the dish and present with a prepared

potato or creamed spinach.

7. Note: This formula can likewise be utilized to cook ribeye,
    T-bone or Porterhouse steaks.

Nutritional Info: Calories: 840, Sodium: 235mg, Dietary Fiber: 0g, Total Fat: 35.4g, Total Carbs: 0.4g, Protein: 123.1g.

Sous Vide Barbecue Tri Tip

SERVINGS: 6-8 | PREP TIME: 15 MINUTES | COOK TIME: 6 HOURS

Tri tip is a magnificent cut of hamburger that is simply starting to become well known so it tends to be precarious to sort out precisely how to cook it. This formula will tell you the best way to make totally delicious medium uncommon tri tip in your sous vide.

INGREDIENTS:

1 (2-3 pounds) tri tip steak
1 tablespoon salt
1 tablespoon dark
pepper 2 teaspoons bean
stew powder
2 teaspoons ground
mustard 1/2 cup grill
sauce

INSTRUCTIONS:

1. Set your Anova to 130F/54.4C.
2. Rub the tri tip with the salt, pepper, bean stew powder, and mustard.
3. Place in a vacuum-fixed pack and lower in the water shower for
    6 hours
4. When the tri tip is almost completed in the water shower, heat your
    oven to high.
5. Remove the tri tip from the sack and coat generously with grill sauce.
    Cook for around 10 minutes or until the grill sauce starts to frame a
    light outside. For a thicker outside layer, rehash this progression with
    extra grill sauce.
6. Remove from oven and cut contrary to what would be expected to
    serve.

Nutritional Info: Calories: 370, Sodium: 1130mg, Dietary Fiber: 0.6g, Total

Sous Vide Pulled Beef

This grill most loved gets its tumble off-the-bone delicacy from a long low cook, and the interesting mix of flavors makes it truly come alive.

INGREDIENTS:

2 pounds meat
brisket 4 twigs of
thyme
1 tablespoon olive oil
2 cloves garlic,
crushed 1 straight leaf
1 yellow onion, chopped
1 enormous ancho bean stew,
cultivated and split 1 tablespoon
tomato paste
1 tablespoon salt
1/4 cup your cherished grill sauce 4
Kaiser rolls or cheeseburger buns

INSTRUCTIONS:

1. Set your Anova to 185F/85C.
2. In a huge cast iron skillet, heat the oil over medium-high hotness and singe the brisket on all sides.
3. In a vacuum-fixed pack, consolidate the hamburger, thyme, garlic, sound leaf, onion, stew, tomato glue, and salt. Seal and lower in the water shower for 24 hours.
4. Remove the pack from the water shower and eliminate the hamburger from the sack, disposing of any remaining fixings. Place the hamburger in an enormous bowl and shred with forks.
5. Serve on the rolls with a liberal spoonful of grill sauce.

Sous Vide Beef Gyros

This Greek propelled wrap is basic however delectable on account of impeccably cooked meat and a perfect proportion of seasoning.

INGREDIENTS:

1 pound sirloin steak
2 tablespoons olive
oil 2 tablespoons
yogurt
1 cucumber, sliced
2 tablespoons lemon
juice 2 tablespoons salt
2 tablespoons dark
pepper 4 huge pita breads

INSTRUCTIONS:

1. Set your Anova to 130F/54C.
2. Rub the hamburger with the salt and pepper and spot in a vacuum-fixed sack with the olive oil. Seal the sack and spot in the water shower for 3 hours.
3. While the hamburger is cooking, join the yogurt, cucumber, and lemon juice.
4. When the meat is done cooking, eliminate from the pack and cut against the grain.
5. Place 1/4 of the hamburger on every pita bread and top with the yogurt sauce. Wrap and serve immediately.

Nutritional Info: Calories: 462, Sodium: 3894mg, Dietary Fiber: 2.6g, Total Fat: 15.1g, Total Carbs: 38.9g, Protein: 41.2g.

CHAPTER 15
DESSERTS

Sous Vide Dulce de Leche

SERVINGS: 12 | PREP TIME: 5 MINUTES | COOK TIME: 12 HOURS

This fixing can be hard to make since it depends vigorously on getting the temperature spot on. Fortunately, your Anova takes all of the mystery out of it by keeping an entirely reliable temperature consistently. Utilize this formula as a garnish for frozen yogurt, cake or any treat really.

INGREDIENTS:

1 can improved dense milk

INSTRUCTIONS:

1. Set your Anova to 185F/85C.
2. Pour the consolidated milk into a vacuum-fixed pack and lower for 12 hours.
3. Remove the sack from the water shower and promptly lower in an ice water shower for 30 minutes. It tends to be utilized quickly or put away in the fridge for later.

Nutritional Info: Calories: 80, Sodium: 32mg, Dietary Fiber: 0g, Total Fat: 2.2g, Total Carbs: 13.6g, Protein: 2.0g.

Sous Vide Vanilla Poached Pears

SERVINGS: 2 | PREP TIME: 10 MINUTES | COOK TIME: 1 HOUR

This solid sweet formula is not difficult to make and packs complex flavor as it cooks.

INGREDIENTS:

2 pears, divided and
cored 1 lemon, halved
2 tablespoons unsalted
margarine 2 tablespoons
sugar
1 teaspoon vanilla glue or extract

INSTRUCTIONS:

1. Set your Anova to 185F/85C.
2. Mix the spread, sugar, and vanilla, and add to a vacuum-fixed sack. Add the pear parts and seal the bag.
3. Submerge the pack in the water shower and cook for 1 hour.
4. Remove the sack from the water and eliminate the pears. Cut the pears and sprinkle the fluid from the pack over them to serve.

Nutritional Info: Calories: 282, Sodium: 85mg, Dietary Fiber: 7.3g, Total Fat: 11.9g, Total Carbs: 46.8g, Protein: 1.2g.

Sous Vide Caramel Apple Rice Pudding

SERVINGS: 6 | PREP TIME: 30 MINUTES | COOK TIME: 45 MINUTES

This rice pudding is upgraded with a rich caramel apple decrease that will please your visitors and makes certain to be impeccably cooked.

INGREDIENTS:

2 tablespoons butter
2 apples, diced
1 cup arborio rice
1 teaspoon cinnamon
1/2 teaspoon ground
ginger 1/4 teaspoon salt
1-1/2 cups
cream 1 cup
milk
1/2 cup caramel syrup

INSTRUCTIONS:

1. Set your Anova to 183F/84C.
2. In an enormous bowl, combine as one the margarine, apples, rice, cinnamon, ginger, salt, cream, milk, and caramel syrup.
3. Pour the combination into a vacuum-fixed sack and lower in the water shower for 45 minutes.
4. When the pudding is done cooking, fill a bowl and cushion with a fork prior to splitting between more modest dishes. The pudding can be served warm, or chilled in the refrigerator.

Nutritional Info: Calories: 250, Sodium: 167mg, Dietary Fiber: 2.6g, Total Fat: 8.3g, Total Carbs: 40.3g, Protein: 4.1g.

Sous Vide Zabaglione

SERVINGS: 4 | PREP TIME: 20 MINUTES | COOK TIME: 30 MINUTES

This Italian treat is far beyond a custard. Cooking in your Anova will draw out each of the unobtrusive flavors for a delightful treat without a great deal of work.

INGREDIENTS:

4 egg yolks
1/2 cup champagne or other shining white wine
1/2 cup weighty whipping cream
1/2 powdered sugar

INSTRUCTIONS:

1. Set your Anova to 165F/74C.
2. Beat the eggs and add the sugar. Blend until the eggs have thickened and afterward add the champagne.
3. Pour the combination into a vacuum-fixed sack and lower in the water shower for 20 minutes.
4. While the blend cooks, whip the weighty cream until stiff.
5. Remove the combination from the water shower and fill a huge bowl. Refrigerate until the combination is cool.
6. Remove the bowl from the fridge and overlay in the whipped cream. Serve immediately.

Nutritional Info: Calories: 603, Sodium: 15mg, Dietary Fiber: 0g, Total Fat: 10.2g, Total Carbs: 125.7g, Protein: 3.0g.

Sous Vide Rich Chocolate Mousse

SERVINGS: 6 | PREP TIME: 30 MINUTES | COOK TIME: 30 MINUTES

This exemplary mousse is rich and debauched yet easy to make. Dazzle your visitor or yourself with the ideal outcomes and scrumptious kind of this lasting favorite.

INGREDIENTS:

8 egg yolks
1 cup sugar
1/4 teaspoon salt
1/2 cup dry marsala wine
1/3 cup unsweetened
cocoa
1/4 cup weighty whipping cream

INSTRUCTIONS:

1. Set your Anova to 165F/74.4C.
2. In a huge bowl combine as one the egg yolks, sugar, salt, and marsala wine.
3. Stir in the cocoa powder and weighty cream and blend until well blended.
4. Pour the combination into a vacuum-fixed sack and lower in the

water shower for 15 minutes.

5. Remove from the water shower and back rub the blend to ensure it remains equitably blended. Supplant the pack in the water shower and cook 15 extra minutes.
6. Remove the sack from the water shower and spoon the mousse into individual dishes. Serve warm or refrigerate for a cold mousse.

Nutritional Info: Calories: 242, Sodium: 111mg, Dietary Fiber: 1.6g, Total Fat: 8.5g, Total Carbs: 37.4g, Protein: 4.6g.

Sous Vide Cinnamon Custard

SERVINGS: 4 | PREP TIME: 20 MINUTES | COOK TIME: 1 HOUR

This light custard is upgraded with a dash of cinnamon. Your Anova will guarantee that the consistency of the custard comes out perfectly.

INGREDIENTS:

3 egg yolks
1/2 cup entire
milk 1/2 cup
cream
4 tablespoons sugar
1/4 teaspoon vanilla
concentrate 1/4 teaspoon
cinnamon
5 graham saltines (discretionary for topping)

INSTRUCTIONS:

1. Set your Anova to 185F/85C.
2. In a medium bowl, join the egg yolks, milk, cream, sugar, vanilla, and cinnamon. Mix well.
3. Pour the blend into a vacuum-fixed bag.
4. Submerge the sack in the water shower for 1 hour.
5. Remove from the water shower and serve. A straightforward garnish for the custard can be made by beating 5 graham saltines in a food processor a few times.

Nutritional Info: Calories: 198, Sodium: 134mg, Dietary Fiber: 0.6g, Total Fat: 7.8g, Total Carbs: 28.4g, Protein: 4.5g.

Sous Vide Lemon Cheesecake

SERVINGS: 6 | PREP TIME: 30 MINUTES | COOK TIME: 90 MINUTES

Cheesecake is one of the most wanton treats out there, and it very well may be made effectively in your Anova. This formula acquaints a smidgen of lemon with give your cheesecake a new finish.

INGREDIENTS

For Crust:
1/2 teaspoon margarine for lubing the ramekins 1/4 cup squashed graham crackers 2 tablespoons dissolved spread 1/2 tablespoon sugar

For Filling:
12 ounces cream cheddar 1/2 cup sugar 1/4 cup harsh cream 2 eggs Zest of one lemon, slashed 2 tablespoons lemon juice

INSTRUCTIONS:

1. Set your Anova to 176F/80C.
2. Grease the ramekins with butter.
3. In a bowl, consolidate all of the outside layer fixings and blend well.
4. Spoon equivalent measures of the covering into every ramekin and press it to the bottom.
5. In another bowl, combine as one the recording fixings utilizing a stand blender or hand mixer.
6. Pour the documenting equally into the ramekins.
7. Place the ramekins one next to the other in a vacuum-fixed sack and try to keep it level. Seal the sack and spot in the water shower for 90 minutes.
8. Remove the pack from the water and eliminate the ramekins from the

pack. Allow the cakes to cool at room temperature for 1 hour and afterward cool further in the cooler. Serve chilled.

Nutritional Info: Calories: 361, Sodium: 245mg, Dietary Fiber: 0g, Total Fat: 27.8g, Total Carbs: 23.4g, Protein: 6.9g.

Sous Vide Crème Brulee

SERVINGS: 4 | PREP TIME: 30 MINUTES | COOK TIME: 2 HOURS

Crème Brulee is a rich sweet that can be made in your Anova with very little work. They can be served plain or finished off with occasional berries.

INGREDIENTS:

2 cups weighty whipping
cream 4 egg yolks
1/4 teaspoon
salt 1/3 cup
sugar

INSTRUCTIONS:

1. Set your Anova to 190F/87.8C.
2. In a little pot, carry the weighty cream to a light bubble and eliminate from heat.
3. Beat the eggs, and gradually add the sugar and salt. Add the cream and blend well.
4. Pour the combination equally into 4 ramekins and spot ramekins inside a vacuum-fixed bag.
5. Seal the pack and spot level at the lower part of the water shower. Cook for 90 minutes.
6. Remove from the water shower and permit to cool for the time being in the refrigerator.
7. Remove from the cooler and sprinkle every ramekin with a light covering of sugar.
8. Heat your grill to high and cook until the top has caramelized. Or on the other hand utilize a blow light to caramelize the sugar. Serve warm.

Nutritional Info: Calories: 375, Sodium: 253mg, Dietary Fiber: 3.8g, Total Fat: 12.4g, Total Carbs: 60.4g, Protein: 6.2g.

Sous Vide Poached Peaches

SERVINGS: 4 | PREP TIME: 10 MINUTES | COOK TIME: 30 MINUTES

A sound choice to peach pie, this poached peach formula will feature the sweet and fragile kind of a peach.

INGREDIENTS:

2 peaches, halved
1 tablespoon dried
lavender 1/4 cup water
1/4 cup honey
1/4 teaspoon
salt

INSTRUCTIONS:

1. Set your Anova to 185F/85C.
2. Place the peaches in a vacuum-fixed pack and pour in the water, honey, lavender, and salt.
3. Seal the sack and lower in the water shower for 20 minutes.
4. Remove the sack from the water shower and spot in the fridge for 1 hour.
5. To serve, place one half peach in each bowl and top with the thickened cooking liquid.

Nutritional Info: Calories: 84, Sodium: 149mg, Dietary Fiber: 0.8g, Total Fat: 0.1g, Total Carbs: 22.1g, Protein: 0.5g.

Sous Vide Blueberry Lemon Compote

SERVINGS: 6 | PREP TIME: 10 MINUTES | COOK TIME: 2 HOURS

This compote can be eaten as all alone as a sound sweet or utilized as a garnish for pound cakes or cheesecakes.

INGREDIENTS:

2 cups new
blueberries 1/2 cup
sugar
Zest of 1 lemon
2 tablespoons lemon
juice 1 tablespoon butter

INSTRUCTIONS:

1. Set your Anova to 185F/85C.
2. In a huge bowl, consolidate the blueberries, sugar, lemon zing and squeeze, and margarine. Blend well.
3. Pour into a vacuum-fixed pack and lower in the water shower for 2 hours.
4. Remove the sack from the water shower and fill a bowl. Mix and either utilize warm or refrigerate for later use.

Nutritional Info: Calories: 111, Sodium: 15mg, Dietary Fiber: 1.5g, Total Fat: 2.2g, Total Carbs: 24.7g, Protein: 0.5g.

Sous Vide Key Lime Custard with Graham Cracker Crumble

SERVINGS: 6 | PREP TIME: 30 MINUTES | COOK TIME: 30 MINUTES

This deconstructed key lime pie is not difficult to make with your Anova, and more grounded than a conventional pie.

INGREDIENTS:

4 egg yolks
4 ounces key lime juice
1 can improved dense milk 2
tablespoons brown sugar
6 graham crackers
2 tablespoons margarine, melted

INSTRUCTIONS:

1. Set your Anova to 180F/82C.
2. In an enormous bowl, consolidate the lime juice, consolidated milk,

and egg yolks.

3. Pour the blend into a vacuum-fixed sack and lower in the water shower for 30 minutes.
4. While the custard cooks, place the graham wafers in a food processor with the earthy colored sugar and spread. Beat until combined.
5. Remove the custard from the water shower and spot in the cooler until cool.
6. To serve, spoon the custard into individual dishes and top with the graham saltine crumble.

Nutritional Info: Calories: 306, Sodium: 182mg, Dietary Fiber: 0g, Total Fat: 12.6g, Total Carbs: 42.9g, Protein: 6.8g.

Sous Vide Toffee Pudding

SERVINGS: 6 | PREP TIME: 20 MINUTES | COOK TIME: 3 HOURS

This customary English most loved can require time and expertise to consummate, however your Anova will transform you into an expert on your first attempt.

INGREDIENTS:

5 tablespoons butter
1 teaspoon baking soda
1 teaspoon baking
powder 1 cup hot water
1/2 cup light earthy
colored sugar 2 eggs,
beaten
1-1/4 cups flour

INSTRUCTIONS:

1. Set your Anova to 195F/91C.
2. Grease 6 ramekins with a tablespoon of butter.
3. In a food processor, cream the spread until feathery, add the eggs each in turn, then, at that point, add the flour and baking powder.
4. Stir in the hot water and baking pop and blend well.
5. Divide the combination equally between the ramekins and spot them level in a vacuum-fixed bag.
6. Seal the pack and lower level on the lower part of the water

shower for 3 hours.

7. When the puddings are done, eliminate from the water shower and cautiously eliminate every pudding from its ramekin. Serve warm or refrigerate and serve later.

Nutritional Info: Calories: 247, Sodium: 305mg, Dietary Fiber: 0.7g, Total Fat: 11.3g, Total Carbs: 32.2g, Protein: 4.7g.

CHAPTER 16
Bonus: Rubs and Seasonings for Sous-Vide Masterpieces

The Ultimate Rub For Ribs, Pulled Pork, or Steaks

This is an incredible conventional rub that can be utilized for either pork shoulder, ribs or even steaks. Essentially blend the fixings and rub generously all around the meat before vacuum sealing.

INGREDIENTS:

1/2 cup paprika
1/3 cup dull earthy
colored sugar 1/4 cup
fit salt
2 tablespoons granulated
garlic 1 tablespoon celery salt
1 tablespoon bean stew powder
1 tablespoon newly ground dark pepper
2 teaspoons onion powder
2 teaspoons dried thyme
2 teaspoons dried
oregano
2 teaspoons mustard
powder 1 teaspoon celery
seed
1/2 teaspoon cayenne pepper

INSTRUCTIONS:

1. Combine all fixings and rub generously on the meat.
2. For the most powerful flavor, apply rub and refrigerate for 2 hours
    before cooking.

Herbed Oil Marinade for Fish and Chicken

The olive oil will make either chicken or fish more delicate, and a basic mix
of fragrant spices will secure magnificent flavor.

INGREDIENTS:

1/2 cup additional virgin olive oil.
1 tablespoon new slashed rosemary
1 tablespoon new hacked thyme
1 teaspoon new cleaved oregano
1/2 teaspoon slashed garlic
1 teaspoon legitimate salt
1/2 teaspoon ground dark
pepper 1 tablespoon dry white
wine
2 teaspoons entire grain mustard

INSTRUCTIONS:

1. Combine all fixings and use to marinate fish or chicken.
2. For best outcomes, don't marinade for longer than 3 hours before cooking.

Smokey Pepper Marinade for Steaks and Chops

Get that smoky barbecued flavor with steaks and hacks and a peppery kick that will make the meat truly come alive.

INGREDIENTS:

1/2 cup
water 1/2
cup beer
3 tablespoons ground dark
pepper 2 teaspoons cayenne
pepper
1 teaspoon ground
mustard 1 tablespoon
cleaved garlic 1
tablespoon fit salt
1 teaspoon fluid smoke

INSTRUCTIONS:

1. Combine all fixings and use to marinade meat for something like 60 minutes, yet not over 3 hours before cooking.

Hollandaise Held at The Perfect Temperature

INGREDIENTS:

1 tablespoon lemon juice
1 stick (8 tablespoons) butter
3 egg yolks
1/2 teaspoon salt

INSTRUCTIONS:

1. Set your Anova to 149F/65C.
2. Combine all fixings and blend well. Place in a vacuum-fixed pack and lower in the water shower for 45 minutes.
3. Remove from the water shower and pour in a blender. Blend until smooth. The sauce can be served quickly or emptied once again into the vacuum-fixed pack and held in the water shower for as long as 3 hours.

www.ingramcontent.com/pod-product-compliance
Lightning Source LLC
Chambersburg PA
CBHW030333160726
47992CB00005B/2252